LIGHT OF GLORY

Children's Stories on the Early Days of the Unification Church

Linna Rapkins

FAMILY FEDERATION
FOR A HEAVENLY USA

The Holy Spirit Association for the Unification of
World Christianity
© 1995, 2018 by HSA Publications

Edited by June Saunders with contributions by Vicki Henry, Larry Moffatt, Nora Spurgin, Barbara Pavey, Ken Weber, Chris Garcia, Sandra Lowen and Rene Balise

All rights reserved. No part of this book may be reproduced or transmitted in any form or by any means, electronic or mechanical, without permission in writing from the publisher, except by a reviewer who may quote brief passages in a review.

ISBN 978-0-910621-78-6

Original versions of the stories in this book appeared in issues of the Blessing Quarterly, published by HSA-UWC.

Cover design: Leehee Wolf

Printed in the United States of America

From the Publisher

Light of Glory is a collection of fictional stories that follow the lives of True Parents, the Rev. Dr. Sun Myung Moon and his wife, Dr. Hak Ja Han Moon, the founders of the Unification Church. Though these stories are not factual, they represent the spirit and experiences of True Parents in their youth.

The book is written in four parts with each part referring to True Parents by both their birth names—Sun Myung Moon and Hak Ja Han—and by their respective titles, as they changed throughout their lives. The four parts are:

Part 1: The Early Years
Part 2: Sun Myung Moon Begins His Ministry
Part 3: The Early Days of the Unification Movement
Part 4: Our True Parents

True Father was called "Sun Myung Moon" or just "Mr. Moon" in his early years into adult hood and then later called "Teacher Moon" when he began his ministry in the 1950's in North Korea. Unificationists have since called him "True Father" and his wife, "True Mother". Eventually, together they came to be known as True Parents. The decision to re-release Light of Glory was made to introduce the heart of True Parents to a new generation of readers, in light of their ongoing ministry.

Contents

From the Publisher.................................3
Foreword 7
Introduction....................................9

Part 1: The Early Years 15
The Boy and the Bully 17
A Most Unusual Child............................20
The Unusual Boy and the All-Night Weasel 24
A Teenager Hears God's Voice 28
Loving One's Enemy: Sun Myung Moon Goes to Japan ...34
A Princess is Born................................42
A Mother's Grief Turns To Joy 49

Part 2: Sun Myung Moon Begins His Ministry.........53
The Message Goes North..........................55
A "Trial" in Pyongyang............................61
The Dungeons of Hell 65
Mountain Tigers..................................73
Refugees..78
Journey to Pusan 86
Life in Pusan 92

Part 3: The Early Days of the Unification Movement ...99
A House Built On Rock...........................101
A Little Peace 110
The Grandmother 119
The Missionary 124
The First Pioneer 129

An Island of Purity..................................135
The Crippled Teacher.............................140
The Unification Church is Born....................147
An Encounter with Ehwa University 157
Jailed 164
The Princess.....................................173
The First 40-Day Condition 177

Part 4: Our True Parents 187
The Bridegroom..................................189
The Marriage of the Lamb 198
Mother's Course..................................204

Foreword

As elder Unificationists of the Family Federation for World Peace and Unification, Linna Rapkins and I shared many responsibilities, especially those connected to youth and education.

When we decided to write and publish individual stories about our True Parents' lives I envisioned that someday the stories would be published together in a book. I remember telling Linna that if she could do a few stories every three months that she would have this book.

I know how much these stories meant to Linna. She would carefully research every piece of church literature and then edit and re-edit until she felt she had done her best. She wanted these stories to be historically correct and interesting enough to hold a child's attention. I know Linna's heart-felt desire to pass the tradition on to the future generations—the tradition that you will read in this book was, in many cases, oral and appeared in print for the first time in the 1980s and 1990s. Before her Seunghwa, I promised Linna that I would do my best to see their publication in one volume.

She was grateful she had been able to write what she had and wished she could have done more; especially, she felt the desire to continue perfecting the stories and adding new tidbits as she came across them. I am still moved to tears by my dear friend, her dedication to our movement of peace and to the Unification faith traditions; to the nurturing of her own faith and for her implicit trust and hope in our future generations. I can see her at her desk now, still trying to fix one last detail as this book goes to press!

May Linna's hopes and our Heavenly Parent's Blessings be with you as you read.

Mrs. Nora Spurgin, 1995

Introduction

A Christmas Story

You have probably heard about the birth of Jesus Christ, the Messiah, in Israel long ago. You have probably heard that when Jesus was born, a beautiful star appeared and shone over the stable. You have heard that angels appeared to shepherds, and heavenly trumpets sounded to announce his birth. Even the animals in the stable knew who Jesus was and bowed down to the newborn Lord of Creation. Many people, including three foreign kings, came to visit baby Jesus and brought him gifts.

These things really happened, but not everyone saw the star or heard the angels and the trumpets. Only a few people did. Most of the world never heard about Jesus until hundreds of years later.

At the time of Jesus' birth, Israel was a very small, not-so-important country. People lived a life based mostly on farming and raising animals. They did not have heat or running water. Israel was not even a free nation—it was under the rule of the Roman Empire. The Israelites could not speak or act as they wanted to; they had to obey Rome.

Like ancient Israel, Korea in 1920 was a small, rural nation and not-so-important in the eyes of the world. Korea was not free either—it was under the harsh rule of old Japan.

When Rev. Sun Myung Moon, our True Father, was born on a farm in 1920 in what is now North Korea, there is no doubt that the angels sang joyful songs, and a few people probably heard and saw them. Perhaps there was a shining star over the farmhouse with the straw roof where he was born. Perhaps the farm animals were restless and happy, knowing that a true lord of creation was born at last. But the real miracle is that a man of true love was born. Like Jesus, Sun Myung Moon felt sorry for all the unhappy people in this world, and he wanted to help them find the light of God's love.

We really do not know much about True Father's birth and childhood, just as we know very little about Jesus' early life. We do know that True Father was born in a year of famine. That means that the farmers' crops did not grow as well as they usually did, and people were very hungry. True Father said that he was always hungry as a boy and remained so until he turned 20-years-old. Yet we know that True Father and his father, and his father before him, often gave their food away to people who were poorer and hungrier than they. His father and grandfather especially favored assisting beggars. Whenever a beggar came to their door, he was fed the best food they had, even if it meant they themselves had to go hungry. There is an old saying that you should be nice to a beggar or stranger because it may be God in disguise—and the Moon family certainly seemed to believe that! They served every beggar as if he were royalty.

True Father came from a family who believed very strongly in freedom. On March 1, 1919, the year before True Father was born, the Korean people bravely rose up against the Japanese to try to free their nation from Japan's rule.

Japan was not like it is today. Today Japan is a prosperous and democratic nation that lives peacefully with other nations and is famous and admired in many ways. But back then, Japan wanted to rule other nations, and Japan was very hard on the Korean people.

Introduction

The Koreans decided to do something about it. On that day, many people turned out in the streets and shouted, "Mansei!" which is a word we also use in the Unification Movement to mean "Victory!" or "One Thousand Years" long reign of a good and righteous ruler. Maybe we can think of it as meaning the same thing as "Long live the King!" But to say "Mansei!" back in 1919 meant that the Korean people wanted to be free, and that made the Japanese rulers very angry. Many courageous and patriotic Korean men and women died that day. Some of True Father's relatives were freedom fighters, so his family on the farm was given harsh treatment by the local Japanese authorities as punishment.

True Father's grandfather was deeply involved in the secret freedom movement of Korea, but he couldn't tell anyone. Everyone thought he'd gambled away the family's money when he had actually given it in secret to the cause of Korean freedom. He was what we call an "unsung hero"—a person who has done great and noble things, but hardly anyone knows about it. In fact, during True Father's childhood years, the children in the family were taught that this grandfather was no good. True Father heard the people in his village say the same thing. It was only later that everyone learned that True Father's grandfather was a great patriot and hero and had been misunderstood by nearly everyone.

True Father admired the kind of person his grandfather was. He thought it was very noble to not speak of all the good things he'd done and to let everyone think badly about him if they wanted to, knowing that someday all the truth would come out. True Father has lived in this way as well.

True Father's parents had thirteen children—a big family, like True Father eventually had—though not all grew up to adulthood. Among all the children, True Father had a special place in his mother's heart growing up. True Father's older brother was the only one of all the other sons that did not die as a child and he once said about True Father, "My brother is more precious than all the world." Why do you suppose his mother and brother felt that way about him? It was because True Father was a shining star of love. Whenever his brothers and sisters felt sick, True Father himself felt the same symptoms, as if he were sick himself. True Father had so much sympathy and empathy for other people, he could feel their pain as if they were his own, and it contributed to his wanting to help people in the world.

Some odd things happened during True Father's early childhood. One time, his mother was spinning some thread, and somehow the wind blew the thread out of the house and it wound around all the trees, like a big net to catch True Father. He saw this as Satan's work. Another time, in a freak accident, a spark from the fire in the house leaped up to the straw roof, and their house caught fire. These supernatural events showed that strong forces were all around True Father. He said that when he went to visit the village, strange things would happen. A cow might suddenly die. A well might suddenly dry up. Wherever True Father went, God and Satan were fighting strongly because Sun Myung Moon was the chosen champion fighter for God and Satan wanted to stop him. Even from True Father's early childhood his family had many unusual things happen to them and they experienced many hardships.

It wasn't much fun to be born like Jesus was—in a cold, dirty stable, without a doctor or warm clothing or even a bed to lie in! A manger, where animals eat their food, is not a clean or nice place to sleep at all. Even though three foreign kings came to see him, they had to hurry away for fear of the bad rulers of Israel. Jesus' life, too, was full of unusual events and hardships.

When Jesus was only twelve years old, he was so smart, his parents found him teaching old men all about God and the scriptures!

Introduction

He could have been a great scholar or political leader, but he decided to live his life for the sake of truth, compassion, and trying to help other people out of their troubles. True Father was so smart in school and so talented in many ways that he could have chosen a career that would lead him to wealth and maybe even fame. He was the first in his class at high school graduation. But, like Jesus, True Father decided he wanted to give his strength and his talents to the suffering and unfortunate people he saw all around him and, if possible, be even more loving than Jesus.

The real miracle of Christmas—greater than any shining star—was the love shining in the hearts of these men. They only wanted to live for the sake of others. Every time we give love to someone else, we are acting like Jesus and True Father and making a small Christmas miracle. That way, every day can be Christmas, if we make it so!

The real miracle of Christmas, greater than the signs and stars, is giving to others with true love in our hearts.

Part I

The Early Years

The Boy and the Bully

Vicki Henry

When Sun Myung Moon was a little boy he understood goodness and wickedness very well. He could not stand to see wickedness. Whenever he saw something bad happening, such as someone stealing or being mean to somebody else, he just had to stop it. Sometimes this meant he had to fight with his fists, even though he didn't want to. First, he would always try to talk with the person who was doing something bad. He wanted them to understand that it was wrong to do those things and to stop doing them. If the person would not listen to him, then he felt he had no choice but to fight.

The only time Sun Myung fought was when someone was being very evil. There could be no room in this world for anything evil because God created it to be a nice place for everyone to live, and Sun Myung wanted that, too. Also, he would only fight someone who was stronger than him, because he felt it would not be fair to fight someone who was smaller and weaker than he.

During his grade school years, there was a very mean boy who always hurt the other children and made them cry. This boy was known to everyone as the school bully, and the smaller children were afraid to go to school because of him. Sun Myung tried over and over to convince him to stop hurting the children, but the bully would not listen. He just laughed at Sun Myung with a very mean laugh.

Sun Myung was only eight years old, and the bully was twelve and much bigger and stronger, but Sun Myung decided he had no choice but to fight this bully. The bully was more than willing to fight because he thought it would be easy to win, since Sun Myung was so young and so much smaller. But Sun Myung knew he was right and that goodness must win over such a wicked person.

The fight began. They fought and fought, punching and wrestling. Sun Myung was hurt very badly, and the fight had to end.

Still, Sun Myung would not give up. Instead, he decided to get some very special training. He would have to become tougher and stronger, so he began going to the mountain above his village. There, he found a strong and solid tree and pretended the tree was the bully and fought with the tree! His fists became sore and tender, but he kept coming back to train until his fists were tough and strong. Sun Myung got so strong that the tree actually broke! He felt Heavenly Parent cheering for him! Now he was ready to fight for goodness.

The next morning, Sun Myung got up, packed his lunch, and set out for school as usual. But when he arrived, instead of going to class, he went to look for the bully. He was not going to let such an evil person do bad things to the other children any longer.

He soon found the bully, marched up to him, and once again told him he must stop hurting the children. The bully just laughed his very mean laugh and did not listen, so Sun Myung decided he had no choice but to fight the bully if the bully was not willing to learn and change.

The fight began. The bully was soon surprised to find that Sun Myung's arms had become very strong, and his fists were hard as rock. Along with that, Sun Myung seemed to have a mysterious power behind him. It was hard to land a punch or get a hold on Sun Myung but Sun Myung Moon's punches always landed, and his grips were hard to get out of. It was Heavenly Parent fighting beside Sun Myung. Heavenly Parent can fight like a tiger when He is defending His children!

The bully had met his match. He had to give up the fight. He knew he could no longer beat Sun Myung. After that, as long as Sun Myung was around, the bully could never hurt the other children or make them cry again.

If you try your hardest to fight for goodness, Heavenly Parent fights on your side.

A Most Unusual Child

June Saunders

It was late at night and Mrs. Kyung Kyu Kim was busily sewing a new shirt for her son. This was her quiet time, when the children were asleep, and she could get many things done quickly. Her life was full of the work of cooking, cleaning, washing, sewing, and all the duties of a housewife and mother living in rural Korea in the 1930s. She had a big family and the work never stopped. Even if she never stopped moving, even when her legs swelled up from standing all the time, there was still more to be done, overflowing into the next day and the next. And most of her tasks were performed with the littlest ones around, pulling on her clothes, asking for attention, for food or drink, making messes, getting into mischief, walking too close to the fire and forcing her to come to the rescue—she felt as if she were going crazy sometimes.

Late at night was the only time when she could breathe deeply, when she could think about things, when the silence and darkness surrounded her, and her little light glowed on. She would sometimes pour herself a cup of hot barley tea, but her fingers worked so quickly, she did not stop to drink any and the tea often grew cold next to her.

This shirt was for her son, Sun Myung. He had given away the shirt on his back again, and there was nothing to do but make him

A Most Unusual Child

another one. She had to admit, this was one habit of his she could do without! She knew where he got it from. His father gave to every beggar that ever came to their door, and his father before him did the same thing. A beggar was like a sacred person to them, and they treated them to the best food they had. Sometimes her husband shouted at her, telling her to serve the beggars faster!

Sometimes she would make something special for the family to eat. It was not easy to make special things for them, and when she did, she would glow with love and anticipation of their pleasure. Then Sun Myung would take his share out of the house and give it away! He always gave it to some unfortunate person who didn't have many treats or enough to eat. When she questioned him about it, he would say, "Is it good or not good to bring food to people in need?" Then she could not say anything.

Well, like father, like son! She could understand Sun Myung giving away his food, but did he have to give his clothes away, too? She made him good clothing, and it took a lot of time. She had plenty of work to do without make him new clothes all the time. Still, what could she say to him? He'd have some ready reply, too smart and good for her to come up with any arguments against it. He always did!

She clucked a little over the stitches. She'd consulted his grandfather about this endless giving of his, and he'd said, "Let him give as he may. He may be a great man someday." So she got no help from that quarter.

Her neck hurt from bending over the small stitches in the dim light, and she shifted her shoulders and stretched. Then a little smile played about her lips. That son! Such an unusual child! He was nothing like any of her other children or any other child in the whole village, as far as she knew. He always had something to say, that was for sure. He came to her every day with many stories. She could not help but listen to him and cheer him on. No matter how exhausted she was, his stories fascinated her, and she found herself saying, "Then what? What then?" as he talked on and on. And she really wanted to know. He'd done so many things already, so many unusual things! He was known all over the village.

He told her how he'd predicted someone was coming down the road before anyone saw them—and he turned out to be right! More than once, too. He told her how he could not sleep at night until he'd made a plan how to beat all the other schoolchildren in sumo wrestling and then carried it out. He told her how he sensed out good and bad places in the mountains and how he'd made arrangements for special privileges with the principal because of his merit. He was always early for school, even though he had to walk almost five miles to get there. He knew when it was going to rain; he seemed to know all about all the birds and animals that lived in the area, their habits and peculiarities. He could foretell whether marriages would work out well or not, and he was so accurate, people consulted him as a fortuneteller to help arrange their marriages!

Yes, he was a remarkable boy, and she listened to him for hours, no matter how tired she was. Then Sun Myung would look at her swollen legs and touch them, and when he saw that the skin did not return to normal for a long time after his squeeze, his eyes filled up with that compassion of his. Then she almost wanted to lay her head on his chest and cry, as if he were her parent, not she, his.

She bent over the material and sewed faster. The fighting worried her. He was always fighting bigger boys who picked on the small ones, and she was afraid for him. She hoped he would grow out of it before he was hurt too badly. She even tried forbidding him to leave the house, but there was no keeping him in. Why, he'd even tried to stop grown-ups from quarreling! It was a wonder he'd never gotten himself into real trouble.

A Most Unusual Child

The people in the village said of him that if he went the way of goodness, he would end up a king, but if he went the way of evil, he would be a most terrible traitor.

Yes, Sun Myung Moon was quite a handful!

Yet she loved him as no mother ever loved a son, she was sure. She hung on his every word; her eyes gobbled up his every expression, hungry with love for him. To her, his face was the finest work of art she had ever seen, and she admired every tilt of his cheek, every pursing of his lips. His eyes, so full of love and sympathy, were like the lights of her whole world. When she was just too weary and all the stresses and strains pulling at her got to be too much, when she felt like telling everyone to go take care of themselves and leave her alone, Sun Myung would say or do something, or she would just see the peaceful look on his face and see how uncomplainingly he managed for himself and tried to do for others. Then she would be comforted, and she would find the strength and hope to go on. He was so sensitive! One time, he had cried for three days straight when he heard about a young boy who had killed himself. Surely someone who cared so much about other people would turn out to be a good person. If only he didn't have to give away his clothes!

She bent over the needle and sought the next stitch with her tired eyes. She could not help herself: she made every stitch carefully, tight and firm, and tugged it lovingly into place, hoping against hope that this time, maybe this time, Sun Myung would keep the clothes for himself.

But she knew he wouldn't.

Even though True Father giving to others made more work for her, Sun Myung Moon's mother had a deep and special love for this unusual child of hers.

The Unusual Boy and the All-Night Weasel

Larry Moffitt

It was winter and a light snowfall had put an inch of fluff over old snow that had turned into an icy crust capable of supporting a grown man if he went slowly and spread his weight along his stride. For a boy of 13, the crust was thick enough to run on without breaking through into the foot of snow below.

Ice crystals sparkled on the moonlit ground like diamonds dropped carelessly through the woods. There was no wind to disturb the delicately formed weasel prints and no sign of wear to indicate whether the tracks had been there an hour or a thousand years. All the boy knew was that he was a half hour into the hunt and that he would go the distance.

The air coming into his chest was cold and dry and when it came out an instant later, it tried to take the lining of his throat with it. His mouth kept filling with mucus as his body rallied to defend itself from the dryness. As he ran, he turned his head to spit, but the wind of running was quicker, and soon a trickle of ice began to form across his cheek.

The hunt wasn't a whim of the moment, but came from the question country children always ask whenever they come upon a set of prints in the woods: Where do the tracks come from and where do they go?

And though he never spoke them aloud, the questions that always filled the boy's mind were beyond those of other children. Where is this weasel going? How many brothers and sisters does it have? He burned to know in detail what this weasel was thinking that could make it run so far. He wanted to know the whole story of this weasel.

There were always tracks of one kind or another around the house, but this time he decided he would follow the clearest set he could find that night. And he would follow them until he caught the weasel.

Thus, within a day, he had told himself; in the morning, I will know better than anyone else where the weasel goes. And I will know what he thinks.

He knew if he were ever to be as wise as Solomon, he would have to do many things like this. And wasn't that his dream? His determination? Someday I want to know everything, he had told his parents. Someday I'm sure you will, they answered. He believed them.

He had been at it for over an hour now, and for the first time, he caught a glimpse of a brownish gray tail as it slid out of sight behind a rock. For the first time since he began, the weasel was aware of him, and the hunt was now a chase.

The sight of the weasel alone was renewal to the boy's energy and warmth to his limbs; hands and feet which had begun to feel the cold and fatigue were forgotten. They, and the other parts of his body, would have to fend for themselves. His mind was abandoning all for the weasel.

He burst up an incline and suddenly found himself knee-deep in an erosion gully that had filled with snow. The animal scampered up the 200-foot run and into the trees beyond, but the boy had to lift his knees to his chest in a slow and painful trudge. He began to crawl on all fours and finally to skim on his belly to keep from sinking. Snow went up his sleeves and into the front of his cloth coat where it melted next to his body, turning his sweat to ice water.

It was three in the morning, and he had been going for five hours without rest. He alternated running with walking but avoided stopping altogether. Because he knew the weasel wouldn't be stopping tonight, he would rest by walking. He told his mind that if running was normal for chasing, then walking was the same as stopping to lie down.

He looked ahead in the moonlight. The weasel was pausing to look behind, trying to understand why he was being pursued as no other had done before. Even a wolf would have stopped before this. There were plenty of other tracks in the snow. Why me? Why doesn't he stop? The weasel stepped on stones across a small creek, leaving four bunched prints atop each powdered mound.

The animal was almost in sight now. It rested whenever it could by walking over deep soft snow to delay the boy. Once, it lay down, looked back, and wearily rose to go on.

The sky in front of the boy was becoming a lighter shade of black. He had never gone so far without stopping, but whenever he thought about resting, he would see the weasel less than 50 feet ahead. For the last two hours, he had begun to feel as if he were touching the animal's fur. He could feel its heart beating in its chest, and when their eyes met, he thought he could see his own face reflected.

By 6:00 a.m., the sun flecked through the trees, and he found himself on a knoll near a village twenty miles from his home. At the clearing's edge, the weasel was lying on its side, breathing heavily, watching the boy's approach. It didn't move as he came closer.

The boy touched its fur, and then knelt beside it to stroke it soothingly from head to tail. The weasel's eyes watched every move, but they were eyes of surrender nonetheless. From so close, the boy clearly saw not his face, but his spirit, reflected in the eyes of the animal. No matter the redness of the boy's face, the blood-laced eyes and the ghastly beard of frozen breath and mucus on his cheeks and chin; no matter his appearance. As the weasel understood the boy's spirit, all panic left it, and its fur lay down on its back, sleek and calm.

In reply to the boy's mercy and in respect for his determination, the weasel's eyes told of its life and gave up its secrets. The feeling of kinship brought tears to the boy. After a time, he spoke softly, "Thank you," and rose to walk toward the village.

He was intensely aware of his hunger, so he knocked at the first house to ask for breakfast. Between bites, he told them who he was and what he had done and why.

When he had finished eating, the farmer's wife smiled and asked, "And what were the weasel's thoughts?"

"He was thinking of me," the boy said.

The natural world of creation, including animals, responds to the touch of a person who wants to understand them and give them love. In fact, they are eagerly awaiting for such people. This story also shows True Father's iron determination and never-give-up spirit.

A Teenager Hears God's Voice

Linna Rapkins

Sun Myung Moon was a teenager; just 16 years old. Even though no one told him to do it, he always got up early to pray before he went to school. He took life very seriously.

One Easter morning he awoke before the sun came up. He put on his clothes and climbed a nearby mountain. Then he began his morning prayer. He didn't pray for new clothes or fancy foods or even a bigger bowl of rice. Instead, Sun Myung prayed for the suffering Koreans. He prayed that he could understand all about God, all about Jesus, and all about the world.

"I pray that I can be very wise so I can help other people," he prayed over and over. "I pray that I can have the greatest faith in all the world. I pray that I can have the most love, even more love than Jesus."

After a long time, something happened that made this the most important Easter of all. Suddenly, standing there before him was a man! He seemed to have appeared out of nowhere.

"Hello," said this man. "Do you recognize me? I am your friend, Jesus."

Sun Myung was shocked he couldn't speak. Can this be true? he thought. Is this actually happening or am I dreaming? Jesus looked

A Teenager Hears God's Voice

real enough, but the young teenager wanted to be sure.

Suddenly, without warning, understanding came to him as like a movie, Jesus' life began to flash before his eyes. Sun Myung could to see all the things that had happened in Jesus' lifetime. He saw how Jesus was born in a stable, how he preached on a mountainside, how he healed the sick, how he died on the cross—everything!

Then Jesus said to him, "I came to earth almost 2,000 years ago to save the world from Satan. I was the Messiah. I wanted to make this world into a beautiful and loving place where everyone could be happy. But they killed me before I could finish my work. Now another person must be the Messiah and finish my work for me. I will help that person. I have come to you today, Sun Myung Moon, to tell you that God has chosen you to be this very special person."

Sun Myung listened very carefully, feeling a bit stunned. He had asked to understand all about God and the world. But to be the Messiah? This was much more than he had asked for. He felt humbled. He took it very seriously.

"This is an enormous responsibility," he prayed with a most sincere heart. "I want to do Your will, God, more than anything else in the world. I do want to live my life for You. But I don't want to take this responsibility lightly. If I say I'll do it, then I must be absolutely determined to really do it." He prayed for guidance. He wanted to understand what God really wanted of him. He prayed for a long, long time. Then Sun Myung began to feel achy and miserable all over. He began to cry. The tears came faster and faster. Soon he was sobbing.

"Oh, it hurts so much," he cried to God. "My heart is aching. I feel like I can never stop crying. Why is this?"

He bent over in pain. He was feeling the pain that had been in God's heart for so long. He was feeling the misery of all the people who had suffered while on earth. He was feeling the pain of the Korean people who had suffered for many, many years. He began to really understand why God needed him so much. He knew he could never turn away from God's sad heart and all the unhappy people in the world.

That day he made a commitment before God. "I will take responsibility for this important work. I will use my whole life for overcoming evil in the world. I want it to be a beautiful, happy garden again." From that moment, no matter how much he suffered or how tired and discouraged he became, Sun Myung Moon never changed his mind. He never gave up; never said, "It's just too much for one man to do." Instead, he always said, "I'm determined to do it."

After that Easter morning, Jesus and God remained with Sun Myung for many years guiding and teaching him directly.

But what should he do first? He said to himself, "I've agreed to finish Jesus' work. But how do I start? He decided to begin with prayer.

Every day he prayed and prayed and prayed. He would often go to a certain mountain to pray. Even when he was sleepy and hungry, he would keep on praying. Sometimes he walked along a riverside—thinking, praying, thinking, praying. He studied the scriptures and searched for answers that would help heal and fix the problems among humanity. He often times felt so desperate, he would kneel down and pound the earth with his fists.

"How do I save these people from Satan? God! Please show me what to do."

He shouted. He cried. "God, who are You, anyway? What are You like? Why are You there? Why did You create us? What relationship are we supposed to have with You? Please, please tell me!" His fists kept pounding the earth. His tears flowed.

Finally, one day, God gave him an answer: "We're supposed to be like a Father and son."

As Sun Myung prayed, he began to understand how important this was.

"Oh, yes! God is our Father. He is Heavenly Father. He is Heavenly Parent! I am His son. All people are His children. That's it! The most important truth in the whole universe! Oh, thank You, my Heavenly Father. Thank You."

Then came his next question. "So what went wrong? Why don't we have a close Father/son relationship? Why aren't we one big happy family? Was it Satan? But who is Satan? Where did he come from? You are only good. Satan is bad. You wouldn't create anything bad, would You?"

"No, I wouldn't," answered Heavenly Father, but He had to leave it up to Sun Myung to find out what had gone wrong.

"How did evil get here? Couldn't You just destroy it? You're all powerful. Why do you let evil stay here? Why? Why? Why?"

Sun Myung asked the questions humankind has been asking for centuries. Maybe you have asked God these questions yourself. God couldn't just tell him the answers, any more than He could answer all those people in the past. God wanted to tell people all the answers, but they couldn't understand the answers or even understand that God was trying to tell them. Some just gave up and said there was no God. There was not enough light in their minds or in the world for them to understand.

Sun Myung had to fight against a lot of spiritual darkness. Like finding a needle in a haystack, searching for the answers to man's age-old questions, Sun Myung felt as if he were in a huge, totally dark circus tent, looking for one pinpoint of light to find his way out. But outside the tent, it was night and darkness, too. Sometimes he felt like he was being smothered, and fear came over Sun Myung in great waves and like great walls.

Sun Myung had to figure things out and then ask if it was true. Little by little, he was able to learn many things about God, about the world, about Jesus, and more.

And he had another problem: Satan. As Sun Myung learned more and more, Satan became more and more worried.

"Hey," he snarled. "If this guy learns about what happened in the Garden of Eden, I'm doomed. I've got to put a stop to this nonsense. Not since Jesus came to earth have I had such problems."

Satan tried desperately to stop Sun Myung Moon. He told him lies. He tried to deceive Sun Myung Moon and make him think there was no such thing as Satan. He tried to tempt Sun Myung Moon to stop his work. He tried to make Sun Myung Moon see how much he would suffer if he kept this up, and how much happier he could be if he just went home. Satan was very, very, very clever, but Sun Myung Moon was always cleverer. He would catch Satan at his tricks.

Satan even tried to beat Sun Myung Moon up. He tried to crush him. He was very strong, and he got other evil spirits to help him. They fought a bloody battle, but Sun Myung was so determined and so strong that he won! Sun Myung Moon had had experience fighting big bullies like Satan, although no earthly bully was ever as tough as Satan.

Sun Myung Moon, really started questioning Satan then. "What did you do against God?" he shouted. "What did you do to Adam and Eve?" Satan refused to answer. He just folded his arms and stared at Sun Myung with an ugly smirk on his face.

So Sun Myung Moon had to guess. "Were you a person?" Satan just shook his head and sneered. "Were you an angel?" Satan looked very angry, but he had to admit that, yes, he was an angel. Sun Myung Moon was too much for Satan. He got more and more of the truth out of Satan. He even began to understand how Satan had felt in the Garden of Eden.

"You must have been lonesome, right?" asked Sun Myung.

"Yes," admitted Satan.

"You must have wanted to be with Adam and Eve, right?"

"Yes!" Satan was squirming.

"You were happier with Eve than with Adam, weren't you?"

"Yes, yes!" Satan was very upset. He tried to escape. But Sun Myung Moon fought with him, made him listen, made him answer. Bit by bit, Sun Myung Moon got the whole story out of him. Satan was furious. Sun Myung Moon had learned all about his secret crime and not even Jesus had been able to do that!

For nine years—starting at age 16—Sun Myung Moon worked to learn all about God's universe. He even learned about spirit world. He was the first person to understand that God had been suffering because of what Satan had done.

"Oh, Heavenly Father," he prayed. "You had no mouth for telling us how You felt. You had no arms for hugging us. You had no legs for chasing after us when we ran away with Satan. If one of Your children was hurting, You couldn't do anything about it. All You could do was feel the pain Yourself and cry and cry. Oh, poor Heavenly Father! I'm so sorry no one could comfort You all these years!"

Over and over, he cried to Heavenly Father, "I'll never leave You. I just want to work for You and make You feel better." Sun Myung Moon couldn't stop crying. Day after day, night after night, he cried. His face became so swollen from the tears that, at times, his own neighbors couldn't even recognize him.

This was all very important to Heavenly Father and Jesus. Sun Myung Moon's tears helped them feel a little better. At last, someone understood how they felt. They loved Sun Myung Moon very, very much.

True Father's compassion for the sorrow of God and humankind helped him to fight against Satan's lies and darkness and bring forth the light of truth.

Loving One's Enemy:
Sun Myung Moon Goes to Japan

Nora Spurgin

It had been three years since Jesus had first appeared to Sun Myung Moon and told him what his mission would be. He had learned many things about God, about the universe, and about Satan. Even though he was spending many hours each day praying, he also went to school. Now Sun Myung was 19 years old. He had graduated from high school. He was wondering if God wanted him to continue going to school—maybe go on to college.

While praying on the mountainside, he asked Heavenly Father, "You have given me such a big mission. Now I have finished high school. I always wanted to go to college, but I want to know what You want me to do now."

Everything was so quiet on the mountainside. Every now and then a bird sailed silently through the air. Sun Myung Moon waited quietly for God's answer. Then, deep inside himself, he heard God say, "Go to school in Japan. You must learn about Japan and the Japanese people."

Sun Myung Moon bowed his head even more deeply when he heard this. "Heavenly Father, I will go to Japan. But I will need Your help. I've never been to another country before."

Loving One's Enemy: Sun Myung Moon Goes to Japan

It was quite a scary thing to think of going to Japan. When Sun Myung Moon was 19 years old, Japan and Korea were enemy countries. Sun Myung Moon thought about the Japanese soldiers who came to his town. They never smiled. They only gave orders to the Korean people. The Japanese soldiers made all the Koreans speak Japanese instead of Korean. It was so hard to learn this language of the enemy. It was always a good feeling to speak Korean to his father and mother at home, but Sun Myung Moon had to speak Japanese in school.

There on the mountainside, he thought about all these things. Whenever he felt scared, it seemed that God put His arms around him and made him feel strong and good inside.

He said to God, "I know You do not want the Japanese and Korean people to be enemies. I will go there for You."

Moon went home and began to make plans. He got a big old brown suitcase and began packing his clothes. Then he said goodbye to his father and mother and brother and sisters at the train station in North Korea. He boarded the train. They all waved to each other until the train was out of sight. Whenever Sun Myung Moon thought of God, he could be very brave and strong. Thinking of God helped him to leave his family, for it was a sad parting for all of them.

The train to the docks was a big black train that was very slow and made a lot of rattling noises. The ride took all day long, and there was nothing to do but to look out the window at the countryside. Sun Myung Moon could see much of the southern part of Korea from the window. As the train slowly chugged along, he was reminded how poor the Korean people really were. They didn't have cars or trucks or tractors. The farmers did all the hard work with their own bare hands. He saw them bending over, working in the rice fields. He could see their backs were hurting.

When he looked at the Korean people, he saw that their faces looked tired. They had many wrinkles. Their clothes were old and worn. Even the old people kept working hard. Sun Myung Moon watched a very old grandmother carrying a heavy load on her back. Tears began to roll down his cheeks. He wiped them away, but more and more tears came.

A very nice lady was sitting beside Sun Myung Moon on the train. She saw him crying.

"Where are you going?" she asked him politely.

Sun Myung Moon said, "I'm going to Japan to attend the university."

"Oh, dear," she said. "You must be so sad to leave your home." She patted him on the shoulder, trying to comfort him. She had a very nice face—like Sun Myung's mother—but he kept on crying and crying. He wasn't crying about leaving home. He was crying because the Korean people were so poor.

He said to Heavenly Father, "I know You have a special plan, but why did You choose Korea? It's such a poor country. How can I ever help this country become great?" Sun Myung Moon also felt sorry that the Korean people were like slaves to the Japanese soldiers who were marching around and controlling everything. He knew that God wanted Korea to be free.

"In Japan, I will work to make Korea free," Sun Myung Moon promised.

Finally, the big train chugged slowly to a stop. They had arrived safely, and everyone was glad. Sun Myung Moon still had tears in his eyes when he said good-bye to the nice lady who had sat beside him the whole day. She never knew why he was crying.

Sun Myung Moon got off the train and looked around. Now he had to find the dock and take the boat to Japan.

He asked a man, "Where is the boat to Japan?" The man pointed to the left. Sun Myung Moon picked up his suitcase and carried it

Loving One's Enemy: Sun Myung Moon Goes to Japan

down the long path to the dock. There was the boat waiting to take its passengers to Japan. Sun Myung Moon joined the other passengers on the boat. After the long noisy and dirty train ride, the boat felt so quiet and peaceful. The water was calm as he waved good-bye to Korea, his home, and sailed out into the sea toward Japan.

In his heart, Sun Myung Moon thought, "I must work in Japan so that someday the Korean and Japanese people can be like one family—not enemies." Thinking about this, he sat down beside his suitcase. As the boat skimmed over the waters in the moonlight, the quiet motion of the waters rocked Sun Myung Moon to sleep. God watched over him with love because God knew that his work would be very difficult.

When the boat entered the dock in Japan, the sun was shining. Sun Myung Moon stood on deck, awake and excited, eager to try out his new home.

He was a very smart young man. He was good at figuring out how things worked, so he had decided to go to a famous university in Japan called Waseda University. He planned to study electrical engineering. Every day Sun Myung Moon went to classes and studied with the other students. He couldn't talk about God in Japan because the Japanese did not like the Christian religion. No one knew he had come to help them understand God. Many times, people treated him badly. Sometimes kids said, "There goes that Korean again." He was often very lonely, but Sun Myung Moon soon found ways to make friends. He was good at many things—both playing and working—so people often gathered to watch him. Sometimes they talked to him because they admired how strong he was.

Sun Myung Moon was always drawn to poor, suffering and lonely people. If he sat next to an old man or woman on the train, he never thought of them as old or ugly or dull. He thought of them as his own mother or father and tried to give them love. Most young people don't pay much attention to old people or like to be with them, preferring to laugh with their young friends, but Sun Myung Moon listened to the old people talk and told them about his home, too. He knew that God's heart was closest to the poorest people, the most sad and lonely people.

One day, he was walking down the street, and he noticed a group of beggars by the side of the road. He felt sorry for them. He said to himself, "I will visit those beggars and take care of them."

He walked back to his room and got some rice. The beggars were sitting in the dirt by the street and held out their hands for money or food whenever someone went by. They were so hungry. When they looked at Sun Myung, even their eyes looked hungry. Their bodies were skinny and dirty. Their black hair was long and stringy.

Sun Myung Moon looked at one beggar and said, "Here, I brought you some rice." Hungrily, they grabbed the rice and ate it quickly.

One of them looked up at Sun Myung Moon and said, "Arigato goziyamas." This means "Thank you" in Japanese. They looked surprised that a Korean college student was kind to them.

So Sun Myung Moon became their friend. He brought rice often. One day he surprised them by pulling out a pair of scissors.

"I'm going to give you haircuts," he announced. One by one, they sat on a box and chunks of dirty black hair fell on the street. One man said gratefully, "Now I feel like a person again." That made Sun Myung Moon smile.

When he was finished, he sat down on the wooden box with them. They all told stories about their families. Sun Myung Moon told them that being Korean or Japanese didn't matter.

"We are all one family," he explained. Were they ever surprised to hear that!

They soon began to love Moon very much. It was a funny sight to see—four Japanese beggars and one Korean student—talking and laughing together. Sometimes Sun Myung Moon had to study for a test and missed a day with them. The beggars' day was so boring then. All day they waited for their friend.

"Where is that young fellow, Moon?" they asked. "We sure do miss him."

They always remembered the young Korean who brought joy to their hearts and put food in their stomachs. Their countries were enemies, but they loved each other because they were people. As Sun Myung Moon had learned in the mountain, all people are God's children.

Sun Myung's life was very hard at this time. He had to buy books and pay rent. He also had to buy food. He had to earn money to buy these things. Sometimes when he went to get a job, the manager would look at him and say, "You are Korean. I can't give you this job." Sun Myung Moon was treated like a servant.

One day, he found a job carrying coal from a ship at the dock to a storage place. Sun Myung Moon had to carry the heavy black coal in bags. It made him dirty and tired to carry it. Most people did not want to do such a dirty, hard job. Each time he trudged up the hill with a bag of coal on his back, people laughed at him. Little children pointed and said, "Look at that dirty man." Sun Myung Moon gritted his teeth and kept going.

He said to God, "Heavenly Father, I'm doing this to bring your love to Japan, but they don't know it. Please, please help me to love these people."

Sun Myung Moon wanted to earn money quickly because he had many other things to do. Suddenly, He had a bright idea. If a whole group of people carried the coal, they could get it done quickly. He hurried back to see his friends.

"Hey, everyone," he said. "I found a job carrying coal. Why don't we all work together? Then we'll get this job done quickly. We can divide the pay and we'll all have some money."

"Yes," his friends agreed. "Let's do it."

They all went down to the dock and began to carry the heavy bags. They worked all day. Soon they were covered with coal dust. As the sweat ran down their faces, it made streaks.

"Whew, this is hard work," one friend panted.

"Sure is," another answered, "but if we all work together, it's true that we can get more done than if Sun Myung-san does it alone."

It grew dark, and they kept working. They worked all night. When the sun came up, they worked all the next day, too. Sun Myung Moon kept cheering them on, and it gave them energy to keep going.

Finally, the last bag of coal was in storage. The little group of tired men, their faces covered with black coal dust and streaked by their sweat, walked painfully back to the manager.

"We're here for our pay!" Sun Myung Moon said.

"What?" said the manager, "How did you do it so fast? It usually takes more than a week. What is this—a trick?" He checked, but all the coal was gone from the dock. It was neatly stacked at the storage place.

He shook his head. "I just can't believe it—but here is your pay."

Sun Myung Moon and his friends joyfully divided it. Then each went home with a wad of money in his pocket. Sun Myung Moon ate a big supper and went to the public bath for a good soak. He was dead tired, but before he went to sleep, he thanked God that now he had money to buy food for a long time. He would have some time to do more important things.

Because carrying coal was such dirty work, only the very poor people were willing to do this job in Japan. Sun Myung Moon worked for a coal company. He carried people's coal to their houses all through the winter, and each person paid him for the coal. In this way, he earned enough money to live on.

Loving One's Enemy: Sun Myung Moon Goes to Japan

One cold evening, Sun Myung Moon was carrying coal to the very last person on his route. It was a big building. It was icy cold, and he couldn't wait to get back to his room to warm up. As he waited at the door, he was thinking, Why do people have to be so poor? Heavenly Father wanted us to enjoy the creation and have a good life full of joy and fun. It's because of Satan that people are so poor and miserable. It made him feel very angry with Satan. Then the building manager came to the door. He received the coal from him. He had a kind face. After he paid Sun Myung Moon for the coal, he smiled, reached into his pocket, and pulled out some extra money.

"This is for you," he said.

Sun Myung Moon was surprised. Few Japanese people did nice things for him because he was a Korean. He was touched. That night, when he said his prayers, he thanked God that one Japanese person had been kind to him. He said to Heavenly Father, "Because of this kind Japanese man, it will be easier to forgive all those people who were unkind." Then he went to sleep with a more peaceful and happy heart.

There was another person who was kind to Sun Myung Moon in Japan. She was Sun Myung's landlady. He rented a small room in her house. When he came home from studying, she was always there to welcome him. He would greet her and talk to her about his day. She began to love Sun Myung Moon as if he were her own son. She never knew that Sun Myung Moon was God's special son, that he had a special mission. Sun Myung Moon always remembered her kindness. Because of her, he could more easily forgive the people who treated him badly every day.

So, even in a nation of enemies, Sun Myung Moon made friends!

We are all brothers and sisters under God, our Heavenly Parent, even if we seem to be enemies. Love and kindness can turn an enemy into a friend!

A Princess is Born

Linna Rapkins

In the same province of North Korea where Sun Myung Moon was born, a young woman named Soon Ae Hong was nearing the time when her baby would arrive. She was at home with her parents almost all the time now. This evening, she sat on a small stool making mandoo for supper. She had a brother, but he had left home, and no one knew where he was. Her own husband had also left, so it was just the three of them. As she rolled bits of chopped meat and vegetables into the paper thin flour shells, her thoughts drifted back to her younger years.

"Mother was a good Christian, and she always told me to watch for the second coming of the Lord Jesus," she remembered. "I haven't found him yet, but I feel in my heart that something is happening."

Soon Ae had already belonged to several churches of great significance for the Lord of the Second Advent. The first was that of Mrs. Sung So Kim: the Holy Lord Order.

"I was barely a teenager," Soon Ae recalled. "But how my life changed at that time. It meant so much to me to be her disciple all those years—what was it, thirteen, fourteen—no, fifteen years it was." Now Soon Ae was 30 years old.

A smile came to her lips. "I loved the way they called her Kamsa Halmoni." In Korean, Kamsa Hamnida means "Thank you." When people went to Kim Halmoni's church, they had wonderful spiritual experiences. Then they would all bow and say over and over, "Kamsa Hamnida. Kamsa Hamnida." They started calling her Kamsa Halmoni, which means something like "Thank Grandmother." Many people loved her dearly and came from all parts of Korea to worship in her church.

As the row of crescent-shaped mandoo grew longer, Soon Ae spoke to the air. "Kim Halmoni, how did you learn all the things you knew? You had so many revelations. You taught us that Jesus did not come to die young, but to get rid of Satan and to build a loving world. And you said the Lord will come again, only it will not be Jesus himself, as everyone thinks. A man will be born in Korea!'"

Often Soon Ae felt excited about this, but she also felt impatient.

"Where is he, Kim Halmoni? How long will we have to wait? If only I could read all your messages now," continued Soon Ae as she poured water over the rice and placed it on the fire. She knew that, even though Kim Halmoni had written everything on twelve rolls of paper, eight feet long each, they had been burned by a relative so the Japanese soldiers could not find any evidence against her.

Yes, evidence! Can you believe anyone would want to hurt such a dear lady? The Japanese, who were controlling Korea then, had heard that she was saying Japan would soon be overcome. They didn't like that!

It was a tragic day when Kim Halmoni was hauled away to jail to be questioned. The thousands of people who came to her church couldn't help her, and so she was questioned and beaten for 100 days. It was awful. Soon Ae's heart still burned with pain whenever she thought of it. The soldiers couldn't prove anything, so they had to let her go, but that dear 62 year old lady was so weakened by the experience that she soon became ill and died. It was the end of her church, also.

"It's so sad," thought Soon Ae, wiping at her tears with one hand while dropping the mandoo into the sizzling oil with the other. "Many people suffered terribly to prepare for the Lord's coming, and in the end they died without even meeting him. I wish, more than anything in life, that I could meet him. Even to cook his food would bring such joy."

As she poked at the mandoo with long wooden chopsticks, her thoughts moved forward to Mr. Lee, who had been one of Kim Halmoni's disciples. Soon after Kim Halmoni's death, his wife, Ho Ho Bin, began receiving revelations. Many of the messages were the same as Kim Halmoni's: They should prepare for the Lord; the Messiah would be born in Korea, and so on.

But there was one big difference. When Mrs. Ho prayed, her abdomen started moving, almost shaking, as if there were a baby dancing inside. Mrs. Ho thought it meant the Lord of the Second Coming might even be born from her womb. In any case, it was God's way of telling them the Second Coming would be born of a woman, just as the First Coming, Jesus, had been. As people began listening to her revelations and praying with her, they became known as Bogjoong-gyo (The Inside Belly Church).

Mr. Lee had told Soon Ae about Mrs. Ho's revelation, and she had joined that group.

One day, as Soon Ae was praying, she saw Jesus standing before her.

"Do you love me?" he asked.

"Oh, yes, I do, Lord Jesus," she answered breathlessly.

"Then please cut your hair short, and use it to knit a pair of socks for me," came his surprising answer.

Korean women always wore their hair long. It was their custom, and everyone followed it. No one was different. But Soon Ae immediately got the scissors and carefully cut her long hair. She smiled now as she remembered shaking her head in the wind and feeling so light and free, and the strange sensation of washing short hair—as if there were nothing there. Most of all, she remembered the stares of the people. But it didn't matter. She loved Jesus.

After she knit the black socks, she started helping Mrs. Ho to make clothing and food for Jesus from the time of his birth until he was 33 years old. Of course, Jesus had been dead a long, long time, but he was alive in spirit world, and his heart was still sore. He had been born to be the King of Kings, but he was poor and mistreated from birth onward.

"Poor little Jesus," Soon Ae sighed, remembering how she had felt at time. "He had only swaddling clothes—rags—wrapped around him. Only God kept him alive in the cold stable."

Later, Mrs. Ho's group began preparing clothing for the Lord of the second coming. In fact, they were looking forward to meeting him in person. He wouldn't be wrapped in rags if they could help it. No, sir. They would prepare everything, and it would be fit for a king.

"As soon as I have this baby, I want to return to help Mrs. Ho," she promised herself. "There is so much to be done." But for now she was here in Pyongyang Do province in the village of Sinli.

As she shifted her weight to ease the strain on her back, she felt gratitude for her ancestors who had been so good. That was why she could understand these things. Because of their goodness, God could work with her. No one told her this; she just knew.

"Isn't it interesting, though, that I am the only daughter in my family, and my mother was the only daughter in hers, and her mother was the only daughter in her family? I wonder what it means?" She drained the mandoo on paper as it was finished.

Then her thoughts moved to a more recent event. She had met a young man named Seung-oon Han. He was from another group that was also looking for the Lord. This young Mr. Han had received a revelation saying, "You should marry the daughter of Yoo-Il Hong. If you have a baby boy, he will become the king of the universe. If you have a girl, she will be the queen of the universe!" He had met her, and they had married, and now she was about to have his baby.

The next day, at 4:30 in the afternoon, as the winter sun was about to touch the horizon, the cry of a newborn baby was heard in the house of Hong.

"It's a girl," announced the midwife, and she placed the tiny baby in her mother's arms. The lunar calendar, which all Koreans use, showed that it was January 6, 1943. The new mother forgot, for the moment, about the prophecy that her baby would be queen of the universe. She just felt joy. This was her own baby daughter—and such a beautiful baby at that. They gazed into each other's eyes, and the little princess had her first meal.

When the sun had disappeared behind the trees and the new mother had rested, her own mother brought in a steaming bowl of freshly made algae soup. Every Korean woman knows that this is what you eat after having a baby. Then you share it with everyone else in the family.

As she sat up on her mat to take the soup, she said, "Omma (mother), her name shall be Hak Ja. It means 'White Crane.' She will be beautiful and graceful."

The new grandmother smiled proudly and left her with her soup. Suddenly Soon Ae stiffened with a jerk, almost spilling the soup all over herself. There was someone else in the room with her! Her eyes made out a dark shape, very ugly and foul-smelling. She was frozen with fear. As it began to speak to her, she suddenly realized with a shudder that this must be Satan! She didn't know what to do.

"Soon Ae Hong," he croaked threateningly. "You must kill your baby tonight. If this child lives, the world will be in very serious trouble."

She set the soup down with trembling hands and reached for her baby. "But why?" she managed to gasp. "Why should I kill my little daughter?" She held the sleeping baby very close, protecting her. Satan just had time enough to sneer when Soon Ae's mother walked in.

"How's the—?" She stopped short when she caught sight of the terrified look on her daughter's face as she clung tightly to her baby.

The older woman knelt down by Soon Ae's mat. "What's wrong? What are you doing?' She caressed her hair, trying to help her relax.

The menacing figure had disappeared. Shaking and pale, Soon Ae explained, "Satan was just here, and he said I should kill my baby."

Her mother didn't know what to say. She just continued smoothing Soon Ae's hair. "There, there. Don't worry. Everything will be alright. It was just a bad dream," she added lamely, knowing full well that Soon Ae had been awake.

Soon Ae worried all week. "What does it mean? Are we in danger? What should I do?" She prayed about it and thought about it every day, and she couldn't forget the awful feeling of it.

Seven days later, she was resting on her mat when another figure appeared in her room. This time it was Kim Halmoni from spirit world—Kamsa Halmoni.

"Kamsa Halmoni!" The feeling Soon Ae got was one of warmth and light, comfort and love. What a world of difference between these two visitations!

"My dear Soon Ae," said Kamsa Halmoni. "I have come to assure you that Hak Ja Han is the daughter of God. She will become the queen of the universe. God is her Father, and you are just taking care of her for Him. Do you understand? You should think of yourself as the babysitter or nanny, not her mother." Then she disappeared.

"Thank you! Thank you!" breathed Soon Ae. Now she understood that Satan had lied to her, had tried to deceive her, because he didn't want his world to be in serious trouble. She would keep these words in her heart always and take very, very good care of her little girl—God's little princess.

As soon as she regained her strength, true to her word, Soon Ae returned to her work with Mrs. Ho Ho Bin. While her little daughter stayed at home with her grandmother, Soon Ae sewed clothes all day for the Lord who was to come.

Little did she know that he had already been born in the very same province where her own daughter was born. Little did she know that he was over 20 years old already and would soon come to Pyongyang Do province. Little did she know her daughter was destined to be his bride.

True Mother's mother, Soon Ae Hong, was a devout servant of the Lord. Through her merit and the merit of her ancestors, this most significant child could be born to her.

A Mother's Grief Turns To Joy

Barbara Pavey

It was 1944. World War II was still going on, and Japan was deeply involved in it. Sun Myung Moon had been going to school and working in Japan for several years. Now the time had come to return to Korea.

Wartime is dangerous because there is a lot of fighting and bombing everywhere. You never know when you might run into a battle or get hit by an exploding bomb. In spite of all the dangers, God wanted Sun Myung Moon to return to Korea at this time. Sun Myung Moon loved God totally, so he was willing to follow God's directions even if it meant his life was in danger.

During the time Sun Myung Moon lived in Japan, his mother, who loved him dearly, used to think about him day and night. She was always wondering what he was doing and when he would return home to Korea. Sun Myung Moon loved his mother very much, so when it was time to return home, the first thing he did was send a letter to tell her when his ship would be arriving and exactly where it would arrive in Korea.

His mother was overjoyed. At last her beloved son was coming home! She had been praying for his return for so long, she could hardly believe the time had finally come.

A few days after receiving his letter, however, his mother's smiles turned to tears. She received a terrible message! It said that the ship Sun Myung Moon was on had been bombed by an American B-29 plane and had sunk. She was completely heart-broken. All she could think of doing was to go to the port where the ship should have come in. Perhaps there were survivors.

She ran out the door, out the gate, and down the road. She ran for miles and miles through the countryside of Korea. She never thought about her safety. She didn't notice that she was hungry and thirsty. She didn't notice that she had forgotten to put on her shoes. She didn't notice the pain as she ran over the rocks, or when she landed on a sharp stick. She ran barefooted all the way to the port!

All she could think about was that her son had sunk with the bombed ship. What were the chances he could have survived? He was probably dead! For a mother who loved her son so much, this was the worst possible thought. She was frantic with worry.

Finally, she arrived at the port, panting and holding her side. She pricked her ears up for news. She asked everyone she could find whether they had heard anything. No one had any answers.

Then she got a big surprise! Sun Myung Moon wasn't on the ship that had sunk, after all! Sun Myung Moon was so important in helping God fulfill His Will so somehow, God guided Sun Myung Moon to change ships at the last moment. He had arrived safely at the port in Korea on a later ship.

When his mother saw him coming down the gangplank, she was the happiest mother in the whole world. You can just imagine just how excited she was to see her son walking off that ship, alive and well! She jumped and cried for joy. It moved Sun Myung's heart to see how much his mother loved him. He hugged her tenderly and cried with her.

A Mother's Grief Turns To Joy

It was about a week later, after she had calmed down from the excitement of seeing her son safely home, that his mother noticed she had hurt her foot on a big splinter. It was sore and infected, but she didn't care. She still smiled and sang all day long. That day, Sun Myung Moon learned a lesson of love he could never forget: that the love of a mother or father is truly the greatest love in the world. He could never forget how she ran barefoot over all those miles for love of her son.

Sun Myung Moon reasoned that since God is our Heavenly Parent, His love must be like that, only greater, for God is the Father and Mother of all the lost children. Whenever anyone is hurting or lost or in trouble, God wants to run to help because that person is God's child. Sometimes He can't, because He hasn't enough people on earth to help Him.

Looking at his loving mother, Sun Myung Moon determined more deeply to help God save His children. Because God knew Sun Myung Moon had that kind of heart, God could protect him through many dangers.

Sun Myung Moon loved his mother very deeply, and yet he loved God even more.

The love of a parent for their child is so strong, they do not even notice their own pain as they search for a lost child. All they care about is finding that child safe and sound. God feels that way about all people, all over the world and in spirit world.

Part 2

Sun Myung Moon Begins His Ministry

The Message Goes North

Ken Weber & Linna Rapkins

Sun Myung Moon had a message for the people: God loved everyone and His children and wanted everyone to live in happiness in a pure garden once again, forgetting all their differences. Jesus had come to restore the Garden of Eden on earth. The world could be made beautiful again if we would all work together with God and be His true sons and daughters. But no one was listening to this message. Sun Myung Moon served and loved people and tried to teach them all he had learned about God's heart. He worked hard for over two years in the southern half of Korea, but he could not find even one person who would become a helper—a disciple who would devote himself or herself as totally to God's will as he had.

He cried and prayed for the people many long hours and looked for a way to win them over, but he met one obstacle after another. Finally, he thought of going north.

"There are many Christians in the north, and God has been preparing them to believe His words," he thought. On June 6, 1946, he set off on foot. He walked north and west. Sun Myung Moon was now in his mid twenties when he began his ministry.

Times were still difficult in Korea. World War II had ended, and the Japanese were gone, but now the Soviets had sent their communist soldiers into Korea. They came from the north, and they immediately terrorized the people. They tried to end religion in Korea. They closed one church after another. Many Christians were arrested and disappeared without a trace.

"There is no God, you fools! You must stop going to church! We will kill you if you go to church!" the communist soldiers threatened.

The Koreans were afraid of these terrible men. Many families tied big bundles of their belongings onto their backs and left their homes, leaving behind everything they couldn't carry. They hurried south to get away. Soon the roads were full of refugees, their backs bent over from the heavy loads, their faces wet with tears. Some of them had to leave family members behind who couldn't make the journey.

Sun Myung Moon was walking north. He knew it was dangerous to go that way, but he felt he must go. There were Christians there who were looking for the returning Messiah. As he walked along, he met thousands of poor Koreans heading the opposite way. They looked at him as if to say, "Why are you going that way, young man? Don't you know it is dangerous?" Later he learned that five million people had left their homes to escape from the communists. He wept for them, but he did not turn his own footsteps south to safety. He continued north.

Eventually, Sun Myung Moon arrived in a town called Pyongyang. In this town, there were many churches. After the Japanese had been driven out, the Koreans had quickly rebuilt their ruined churches so they could worship together again. It was such a spiritual place that many Koreans called it the "Second Jerusalem."

When the communist soldiers came, they tried time and again to make these Christians stop going to church, but the Christians loved God and Jesus so much and were so strong that the communists had failed to stop them. Every Sunday morning at 5:00 a.m., the church bells rang throughout the city. At that early hour, prayer meetings were held. Sometimes as many as 12,000 people were praying all in unison. Many had to stand outside because there was not enough room inside the churches. Neither cold nor snow could keep them away.

Sun Myung Moon found a room in a small house with a Christian couple. Wasting no time, he began going to the churches to meet Christians. He invited people to his little room, where he taught them about God's revelation to him. The word passed around rather quickly and more and more Christians came to hear him speak. Many of these people were old women who had received messages from spirit world to go to him. Over and over, hour after hour, day after day, Sun Myung Moon taught from his little Bible. Soon the corners of the pages became worn from the constant use. They began to call him Teacher Moon.

There was one woman who came many times. All her life, she had longed for Jesus to return. She loved Jesus very much, and she had a strong feeling he would come to Korea. She had many questions which were never answered at her church. When she first heard Teacher Moon speak, her questions were all answered. She suddenly felt warm all over, and her heart beat faster. The words vibrated through her body: "This is it! This is it!" She felt so much excitement. After the meeting, she quickly went to all her friends and relatives and told them to go hear this man speak. With great joy, she shared her feelings with her husband, but he wasn't so joyous about it.

"I'm not interested in such a person," he scowled. "And I don't want to hear what he has to say. Forget about him, wife!"

She hoped his feelings would change, so she tried to win him over. She worked harder. She kept the house cleaner and cooked better food. She served him and gave him more love, but still he was jealous because she kept going to see Teacher Moon.

"Why do you keep going to that man's room? Have you fallen in love with him? I think he is trying to take all the wives away from their husbands!" He got together with some of the other husbands whose wives were visiting Teacher Moon, and they looked for a way to stop him from teaching.

"He's a heretic," they told everyone. "We must run him out of town." But Sun Myung Moon continued teaching.

It was only many years later that this man changed his mind. After watching his wife and seeing her great faith and love, he finally repented. He supported Teacher Moon and his disciples and encouraged his own children to learn.

This woman encouraged many people to come listen. One person she encouraged was her 18 year old nephew. He had just graduated from high school, and he went to his aunt's house to ask her advice on what he should do with his life. He respected her very much, so when she told him to go with her to hear Teacher Moon's message, he obeyed. The next day, he went again. And again. He never talked or asked questions because he was shy, and he thought he knew nothing, but he liked to be there because he felt peaceful around Teacher Moon.

Sun Myung Moon looked at him and said, "You meditate a lot, don't you? But you need to focus on one thing." The young man was very surprised because it was exactly true! This person's name was Won Pil Kim, and he became Sun Myung Moon's first full-time disciple. It was July, 1946, forty days after Sun Myung Moon had left the southern half of Korea.

When Won Pil Kim first came to hear Teacher Moon, the July weather was scorching hot, and the room was so small that the heat in there was almost unbearable. Yet Teacher Moon always spoke strongly and with great energy for six or eight hours at a time. (That is like going from breakfast until dinner!) He didn't even stop to rest or eat, and yet he never seemed to get tired. As Teacher Moon spoke in the stifling heat, the sweat poured down his body. Whenever he finished speaking, his clothes were so soaked from the sweat that they looked as if Teacher Moon had just come in from the rain. Often, Teacher Moon would take his shirt off afterwards and twist it in his hands to wring out the dripping sweat.

Won Pil Kim was amazed. "How can he do it?" he asked himself. "He is so strong, so special." He became determined to help Teacher Moon all he could and to be a good disciple forever.

Won Pil Kim always stayed with Teacher Moon when he spoke to the people. He took notes on everything Teacher Moon said and studied them over and over until he had memorized them. Then he could carry the words in his heart wherever he went.

Besides teaching the people who came to his room, Teacher Moon also spent many hours in meditation and prayer, especially on Sundays. He would spend several hours praying, and then have Sunday Service. Then they would all go together to the countryside and talk. It was a time to ask Teacher Moon questions and understand his words better.

"Won Pil," said Teacher Moon one day. "Don't you have any questions? You never ask me anything at all."

"No, Teacher," answered Won Pil Kim.

"I want you to always remember one thing," Teacher Moon said to him. "Our group of disciples is different than any other group in history."

Won Pil Kim understood those words only later, when he realized Teacher Moon was the Messiah for the whole world and the True Parent of all humankind.

As more people came to hear Teacher Moon, amazing things began to happen. Whenever Teacher Moon taught God's truth, the people sat as if riveted to the floor, their eyes never leaving his face. It was as if they had to hear every word. Then something like a heat wave would pass through their bodies. It was like electricity or fire, only it didn't hurt. They got so excited that they forgot their problems and began repenting for all the bad things they had done in their lives. They repented and cried and prayed, and after a while, it was as if some great burden had been lifted from them. They felt as if they had been set free. They would rise up, feeling so joyous and light that they would start dancing around.

The houses were close together in the towns of Korea. The walls were quite thin, and the paper doors were so thin you could see through them at night. When these early disciples of Teacher Moon gathered, they prayed and cried and sang and danced. They were a very noisy group, and everyone in the neighborhood could hear them.

"Who are those people, anyway?" people asked each other.

"I don't know, but there are men and women in there, and they stay together until late at night."

"I saw them dancing around."

"They must be crazy people. Maybe they're dangerous."

The neighbors didn't like anything different going on, so they reported Teacher Moon's group of disciples to the police. The communist police officers didn't like Teacher Moon either. They thought he might be a spy from the southern half of Korea. He had suddenly appeared from the south, and he had no identification with him. Also, the police had just arrested all the members of another church, and now here was this group acting the same way.

In August, not quite two months after Sun Myung Moon arrived in Pyongyang, he was arrested and put into Pyongyang prison. The joy and dancing was over.

True Father paid a great price by going north, into danger. The early days of what would soon become the Unification Church began to bear fruit because of his sacrifice but along with success came persecution.

A "Trial" in Pyongyang

Ken Weber & Mrs. Linna Rapkins

After his ordeal in Pyongyang prison, Sun Myung Moon's disciples tried to make him rest, but all he could think of was returning to his mission. Before long, he was holding long meetings again. He taught the people from his Bible, always speaking very strongly and with many tears.

The meetings were very exciting. The people gave their full attention. They felt they had to get every word down on paper, and they would take notes as fast as they could. They didn't plan to stay late, but when Teacher Moon spoke, they forgot about time; they forgot about their families. Before they knew it, the time had flown by, and it was late at night. The same kind of feelings of electricity came over them, and they just had to jump up and dance around for joy. God's love made them feel so wonderful!

Sometimes miracles happened. Some who came were quite rich, and the food Teacher Moon served was simple. But to them, it tasted more delicious than fancy, rich food. One wealthy man who had a stomach problem was cured after eating the food at Teacher Moon's place. Word got out that Teacher Moon had some kind of "miracle food."

Many times, as Teacher Moon spoke, they learned answers to questions they had been asking for years. Then they would get so inspired and excited they couldn't wait to go out and tell other Christians.

"I'm going to tell my minister all about this," they exclaimed, one after another. "He'll be so excited to hear it."

But almost always, the ministers of their old churches were not excited at all.

They said, "You're wrong. These answers are not true, and anyone who makes their people dance around in church must be from the devil."

Many of them stopped going to their old churches altogether. The ministers became very upset when some of their best members left, so they got together with their own church members and went to argue with Teacher Moon. They wanted to ask him difficult questions and show the people how wrong he was. But Teacher Moon answered their questions before they even asked them!

"Mr. Moon must have special powers," they murmured. "He's surely of the devil. We must stop him."

This is so much like what Jesus went through when he was alive. These are the same types of things the religious leaders said about Jesus when he was preaching, too. These ministers spread the word around that Sun Myung Moon was a bad man. They tried to scare the people. They even went to the communists and accused him of being dangerous.

"This man, Sun Myung Moon, is breaking up our churches; he's breaking up homes," they declared. "He will want to break you up, too. He's probably a spy from the south. You must get rid of him." More than 80 ministers wrote letters to the police, accusing Sun Myung Moon of all kinds of crimes.

This made the communists very happy, indeed. They had already heard that Sun Myung Moon had come back to life and was preaching again. They had started watching him carefully. Their belief was

A "Trial" in Pyongyang

that anyone who believed there is a God is mentally ill. They wanted to just get rid of them all, so they were watching for their chance—for some excuse. Now one church was fighting against another! What better way to make the churches weak? So they helped by spreading even more lies about Sun Myung Moon.

On February 22, 1948, because of the ministers' complaints, Sun Myung Moon was arrested and brought to trial. He had been teaching in Pyongyang one year and ten months, almost two years.

By this time, Sun Myung Moon had become well known in Pyongyang, so the courtroom at the trial was packed with people. He was led into the room in handcuffs and with his head shaved. He was accused of taking money from the poor and using it for himself. He was also accused of telling people lies.

The judge tried to use Sun Myung Moon to make people who believe in God, whom they can't see, look silly. He tried to say that man had invented electricity, which we can't see, so man could also invent a God. He asked Sun Myung Moon some questions about electricity, but Sun Myung Moon was an electrical engineer, and he knew all about electricity and spoke very well indeed. He turned the judge's point around by saying that even though electricity is an invisible force, it still exists. We believe in electricity and know it has power, so an invisible God can exist, too. The judge quickly stopped asking Sun Myung Moon questions!

After the trial, the judge pronounced Sun Myung Moon guilty. Everyone knew it was always best to remain silent. If the judge became angry, he could make the prisoner stay in prison even longer. But Sun Myung Moon knew he had been wronged, so he stood up and asked that the charges be dropped because they were not true. He said he had not told any lies or deceived the people.

The judge was shocked. The communist leaders who were watching had hoped to show that people who believe in God are weak and silly. Instead, this man showed brains and courage! Won Pil Kim was in the audience that day. His eyes filled with tears as he saw how brave his beloved Teacher was. Up until then, he had only seen Teacher Moon's loving and warm side. In the courtroom, he saw a fearless man.

The charges were not dropped, and Sun Myung Moon was sentenced to five years in prison. As he was led away, he looked back at his disciples and smiled reassuringly, as if to say, "Don't lose heart. I'll be back." With his chained hands raised high in a sign of hope, he was escorted off to prison.

Sun Myung Moon's disciples felt totally sad and discouraged at that point. But Sun Myung Moon's face was shining with hope that, through his prison term, God could do great things for Korea.

True Father's courage at his trial showed the communists and audience alike that people of faith are not stupid or weak. A person of true faith, like True Father, is very smart and strong.

The Dungeons of Hell

Sandra Lowen

Sun Myung Moon was sent to the Tong Nee Special Labor Concentration Camp at Hung Nam, a northeastern port city in North Korea. This was not like an American prison, where prisoners might do light jobs and spend many hours in clean cells, writing letters home, relaxing, watching TV, or even working on their college degrees. This prison was at a nitrogen fertilizer factory. There was a small mountain of hardened lime, which the prisoners had to break up and haul to another place. They had to break up the lime, pack it into rice-straw bags holding eighty pounds each, weigh it, and take it off to the loading dock. Each group of ten men was responsible for loading 1,300 bags every day, which meant about one bag every half-minute. The bags were very heavy. The lime made their fingers sting and then bleed with big sores.

You might think a man would simply decide not to work; but this was not possible at the Tong Nee Camp. If the team did not do its work, they didn't get anything to eat that day. In order to live, they had to eat, and in order to eat, they had to do the work. They didn't eat steaks or chicken or vegetables, nor any of the foods we eat to stay strong. They received just one small ball of boiled barley, or a few spoonful's of rice or wheat each day. Even if a person was lucky enough to eat every day, it was still not enough food to live on. Within a few weeks, the men became so skinny you could see their bones. Their bellies became swollen from starvation. Very few prisoners lived more than a year in that place. Sun Myung Moon was sentenced to five years! How was he going to survive?

As soon as he arrived, Sun Myung Moon began planning how he would stay alive. Most people would think the best plan would be to concentrate all your energy on finding ways to help yourself and put yourself ahead of others. That was not his way, because he knew it was not God's way.

First, Sun Myung Moon looked at the food situation. If he became desperately concerned about this little lump of grain, he would surely die. He saw how the people acted around him. One day a prisoner who had been very ill died while eating his meal. When he fell over, two or three prisoners rushed to his side and took the food he had not yet eaten from his bowl. They were so hungry themselves, they did not even think about the dead man.

He decided that instead of trying to find ways to get more food for himself, he would share what little he had with the others. He would divide his little rice ball in half and give one half away to another prisoner. This was revolutionary! People in that prison were so hungry, they would gladly hurt each other to get food for themselves, but Sun Myung Moon was hurting himself to give food to others! He did this for quite some time, and then he felt God tell him it was time to start eating his whole portion himself. By then, Sun Myung Moon was so used to a half portion, the full portion felt like a feast in his stomach!

The time just before the Korean War in 1950 was very difficult even for those who were not in prison. Disciples such as Mrs. Oak and Won Pil Kim were allowed to visit every two months, and they would sometimes manage to bring Teacher Moon a little bag of rice powder. Sun Myung Moon easily could have gone to a quiet corner and eaten the rice powder himself, but that was not his way. He would always share it with other prisoners. Sometimes he filled their pockets with the precious powder when they weren't looking.

One day Sun Myung Moon received a package of rice powder. Before he could share it, he discovered it was missing. The other prisoners became outraged. Who would do such a thing? Finally they found the guilty man and dragged him before Sun Myung Moon, so he could accuse him. Instead, he showed mercy on the thief. He looked at him and said, "You must have been so very hungry to have to steal my food. He who is hungry has the right to eat. Give me your bag." He then poured all the rice powder he had left into the man's bag.

Sun Myung Moon decided to work harder than anyone at the camp had ever worked before in order to conquer the impossible workload. The nine workers on his team found that they could fill enough bags of lime when they worked with him. Soon other prisoners were trying to get on his team. Twice he was given a special award by the communists for his hard work. So, even they, who were on Satan's side, had to admit Sun Myung Moon worked hard!

When a friendly prisoner asked him why he worked so hard, Sun Myung Moon said, "If I work even a little more and a little harder, will it not reduce my fellow workers' burden?"

Sun Myung Moon suffered a lot in this situation. We cannot even imagine how terrible such a prison is. There is no color, no music, no song, no dance—and probably very little laughter or even talking. Everyone just has to concentrate on surviving, and even then, most of them die. Their clothes were dirty, their beds were dirty and hard, their bathroom was a dirty bucket right in front of everyone. Most of the men had lice and fleas and problems with their stomachs. The guards treated them roughly, made fun of them, and said nasty things to them and about them. Even if they were young, the men began to look very old and very tired after only a short time.

Sun Myung Moon would take a small amount of the water they were given to drink and wash himself with it. In some ways, this must have seemed like a waste of water, because you could not get clean in that situation or stay clean. But Sun Myung Moon maintained and protected what pride and dignity he could in his situation because he was a human being; he was God's son; and he had to treat himself with respect, even if he was in a world that was without respect for human beings.

On the outside, Sun Myung Moon looked the same as the other prisoners, just a miserable man in a terrible situation. But internally, he was like a shining light in that drab and dark place. His acts of kindness must have felt like a warm, loving hand patting the men on the shoulder, reminding them that there was a better way to live. Maybe he even reminded them of their own mothers' love, far away in the past. When it was late at night and everyone was sleeping, Sun Myung Moon would talk to God and sing to Him. He never complained to God about his situation. He never prayed to God asking Him to help him or get him out of prison or to make him feel better. His first thought was that God must be suffering so much to see what he was going through. If he acted sad, it would make God suffer more, so he spoke brave words to God.

"I will never give up, Heavenly Father," he prayed with great love. "Please don't worry about me." He also told God he would fulfill his mission; he would be victorious.

The prisoners never got enough sleep, but Sun Myung Moon used his sleeping time to meditate and pray. A prisoner later said that when they went to sleep, they would see him kneeling to pray. When they woke up, he was still praying!

The other prisoners came to love him. Many times, tears came into their eyes because he had touched their hearts so. He could

The Dungeons of Hell

not say one word about his mission to them, or even speak about God or religion at all. The communists would not have allowed it. Therefore, spirit world spoke out for him. Many prisoners were told in dreams that he was a very special person and that they should become his helpers. Even some of the communist guards were witnessed to by spirit world. A famous Korean guardian spirit named Sansilyong would come to them in dreams and tell them not to mistreat Sun Myung Moon, who always seemed to know about these dreams without being told. Many of the guards believed he had supernatural powers and were afraid to be cruel to him. Thus Sun Myung Moon was somewhat protected.

At least twelve prisoners became his disciples. One of these men was named Jung Hwa Pak. Mr. Pak was the leader of a large group of prisoners. Sun Myung Moon was in his group. He tried to give Sun Myung Moon easier jobs and extra food whenever possible, but Sun Myung Moon always refused these favors.

The summers were extremely hot. Sun Myung Moon always kept all his clothes on. Mr. Pak kindly suggested, "Why don't you take off your rubber shoes and shirt? I'll take you somewhere to wash."

But Sun Myung Moon felt that Heavenly Father wanted him to keep his body precious and hidden from others.

At one point, he got very sick with malaria. He could have rested in the sick people's area. Even the cruel communists recognized that someone with malaria could not work. But he said, "No," and continued working, sweating greatly, barely having the energy to stay on his feet. No one else could have survived such punishment.

Sun Myung Moon's number in prison was 596. When this number is spoken aloud in Korean, it sounds as if someone is saying the same word as "Sorrowful." In this way, Heavenly Father expressed how Sun Myung Moon's undeserved punishment made Him feel.

Rumors spread in the prison camp that war was coming. The communist guards of the camp seemed nervous. Something was about to happen.

One day, one of Sun Myung Moon prisoner disciples came to him and said that he might have a chance to work in another part of the camp where the work was much easier. He asked if he should go there.

Sun Myung Moon looked at the man and said, "No, don't go." But the man continued to think about the easier work at that camp. He had been working so hard, his bones were crying out for some rest. When his chance came, therefore, he decided to take it, and he went to the other area.

A second prisoner disciple came to Sun Myung Moon and told him he also had a chance to work at the easier camp down the road and asked what he thought. He looked at the man for a moment, and then said, "All right, go. But if anything seems suspicious to you, run back to this part of the camp immediately." That man also went. A short time later, in June 1950, North Korea attacked South Korea. It was the beginning of the Korean War.

In August, Mr. Pak was released from the prison camp. Before leaving, he asked Sun Myung Moon what he should do.

Sun Myung Moon told him, "Go to Pyongyang, and tell the disciples not to worry about me. I will return soon."

The Korean War progressed, and by October, the bombing began near the Tong Nee Camp. The guards were terrified for their own lives and even more terrified that their prisoners might escape. They decided that they would just shoot all the prisoners so they couldn't escape. They ordered some prisoners from the other camp area to line up and walk down the road.

The second man, who had received Sun Myung Moon's permission to go there, became suspicious of what was going on, and he

The Dungeons of Hell

quickly ran back to the main camp. The first man, who went without his permission, was never heard from again.

The prisoners in the main camp were then herded into their cells. One cell at a time, the men were brought out to be shot. The communists were determined that no one would be spared. Cell by cell, the prisoners were killed. The communists reached the cell next to Sun Myung Moon's and took out all the prisoners and shot them. It was the emergency of emergencies. Sun Myung Moon was next! His life and God's dispensation hung by a thread. Only seconds to go before he would be shot! There was absolutely no escape.

All over Korea, spirit world had battled beside the United Nations fighting men to save Korea and to liberate Hung Nam. They had only one thought: the Messiah was in terrible danger, and the men had to win their battles in order to rescue him. The future of the world depended upon it. Although the men did not know it and thought they fought only for political causes, spirit world was with them. Spirits whispered in the soldiers' ears, sharpened their eyes, gave them courage and the strength to go on fighting. It was all with one goal in mind: save the Messiah's life in Hung Nam. Heaven and heaven's forces fought with tears and fury to try to get the soldiers to Hung Nam on time.

The communist guards called out the numbers of some people in Sun Myung Moon's own cell. The people next to him began filing out to go to their deaths.

Like a lightning storm, bombs began falling on the camp. The United Nations forces had arrived.

Terrified, the communist jailers ran to underground shelters, leaving the prisoners, including Sun Myung Moon, out in the open. Staying alive among the falling bombs was almost impossible. Hundreds were killed, but Sun Myung Moon received a message from God that no bombs would come near him.

He did not say this to his disciples, but he said, "Let us keep very close together. We will live or die together." His disciples and other people gathered around him. Soon others, including some communists, realized that Sun Myung Moon's life seemed charmed, so they gathered close to him, too.

Sun Myung Moon was set free by the United Nations forces on October 14, 1950. He had survived two and a half years in that terrible place. It took him ten days to walk to Pyongyang, and he stayed there for forty days, looking for his disciples.

Why couldn't Satan kill Sun Myung Moon in the camp? Why didn't he die from starvation, hard work, from the shootings, or even from the bombs? It was because he won the victory of love. It was a terrible time for Satan. Satan had accomplished so much through hate. So much evil was in the world because of his hatred. But he was defeated by a stronger force—the force of love. Because Sun Myung Moon had so much love in his heart for God and for other people, nothing could stop or defeat him.

Love triumphed in the dungeons of hell—Hung Nam prison camp. True Father proved that love is the greatest power in the universe, a shining light even in the deepest darkness.

Mountain Tigers

Chris Garcia and June Saunders

If you had been there, you would have seen three people walking among the trees in the moonlight, feeling their way down a small path, talking to each other in whispers. They moved gently down the mountainside through the pine needles. You would have seen that the woman in the rear was fairly old, maybe 60 years old; the woman in front was middle-aged, perhaps in her mid-thirties; and the little girl walking between them down the mountain path was definitely six years old.

The little girl's name was Hak Ja Han, and it was fortunate that she was just the type of little girl she was. By nature, Hak Ja Han was quiet, and living under the communist regime had trained her to be even more quiet. Because she was soft-spoken and such a pretty little thing, even the communist officials felt charmed by her and sold her nice things from their stores, like apples. In this situation, her quietness was a lifesaver, because one wrong move might tip off the North Korean soldiers that people were trying to escape to the South.

Her mother and grandmother were scared as they approached the border area between North and South. They knew all too well what communism was. They had just spent eleven days in prison, and Soon Ae Hong never wanted to see a communist again. Her face was turned southward where freedom—and the coming Lord—awaited them.

She was scared because a neighbor who had tried to escape to the southern half of Korea at night, just like they were doing now, had stepped on a flat metal can buried in the ground of the road and gone straight home to Jesus in a clap of thunder and a flash of light. It was a land mine, a little bomb buried in the ground.

All these things pressed on Soon Ae's heart as she led the way for her little girl and for her own mother. The starry night was full of dangerous things. The mountains were full of soldiers—the soldiers of the South and the soldiers of Kim Il Sung. The sudden blast of a rifle behind a bush might end their business on this earth at any moment. If they met South Koreans, they would probably be safe. If they met Kim Il Sung's army from the North—she did not bear thinking of it.

It was midnight when she had pulled Hak Ja Han out from under her blanket and told her to be very, very quiet or they would all be in a lot of trouble. Hak Ja Han had obeyed without a sound. They slowly walked out of the residential area and toward the border. She felt the intensity of the spirit world all around her as they picked their way through the solid darkness. The sky was filled with stars and a sliver of a crescent moon. The cool night air seemed full of weight and soft winds that sounded like voices talking about them.

"Omma," said the child. "Are there still tigers in the forest?"

"I don't think so, dear," answered Soon Ae and this was true as far as she knew. The farmers and ginseng hunters had said the wild animals had been driven from the mountains by the fighting of men and had gone to look for quieter hunting grounds. But you could never be sure about Siberian tigers, who weren't afraid of anything.

"What about ghosts?" asked Hak Ja Han.

"Oh, probably there are some," said Mrs. Hong, trying to sound

Mountain Tigers

nonchalant. To deny it might draw bad luck. And her mysterious little girl had a funny way of knowing when people weren't saying what they really thought.

"Good ghosts or bad ghosts, Omma?"

"I'm sure they're good ghosts."

"If we pray to God, maybe the good ghosts will protect us from the bad ones."

"Yes, yes." Soon Ae heard the shaking in her own voice and hoped her daughter hadn't noticed it. They were so alone out here! Anything could happen to them, and Satan had tried so many times before to destroy her little girl. She knew they had some great destiny to fulfill for God, and that was why they had to get to the South. Somewhere in the South, the Messiah would be waiting for them. But first, there were many things on the way they had to get through. Tigers. Yes, tigers—tigers with guns, whose hearts were worse than tigers who killed only for food. Those tigers were Kim Il Sung's army. She peered into the darkness and pulled her daughter closer to her.

When they crossed the boundary, Hak Ja Han asked if she could sing.

"And do I still have to sing a song of Kim Il Sung? May I sing the songs of South Korea?"

Before Soon Ae could answer, there was a crack and a flash of fire from behind a tree. It was a rifle. Suddenly the night was full of lights, and still they couldn't see. "Crack, crack!" went the guns, and there were red flashes of light. Grandmother shrieked as a bullet hit the pine tree by her shoulder, spraying her with chips of tree bark. Something hot zizzed by Soon Ae's ear. She had a moment of sheer, animal terror. She wanted to jump out of her body and be somewhere—anywhere—else on earth at that moment. Then her faith awakened in her, and she prayed, "Oh, Father, save your daughter!"

Then a strange sound came to their ears—strange in the midst of this deep darkness and sudden light and fear more real than the air around them. Hak Ja Han was singing.

The sweet little voice wafted on the air of the darkness, singing a song of the South. In the voice was purity, sanity, a reminder of home and family, peaceful villages and the friendly greetings of neighbors. It was a hopeful sound, a wistful sound, and there was a child-like confidence underneath it.

A soldier screamed, "Hold your fire!"

There was silence, and then torches lit up. Soon Ae's chest was contracted into a tight wire cage, and her heart fluttered around in it like a frantic little bird. Was this it?

Lights were cautiously held close to their faces, but whoever held the lights were deep in darkness. The singing ended naturally, calmly.

"Who are you?" a soldier asked gruffly.

"We are from the North. Myself, my mother, and my daughter," said Soon Ae shakily. She thought she detected the accent of a Southern province in the unseen speaker. She risked the words, "We escaped."

More torches came up. They were taken a more respectful distance from the two women's faces, and you could feel the relief of the soldiers. They were too disciplined to sigh, but there was a general relaxation. One torch lit up the face of Hak Ja Han: white, small, oval, and gleaming like a small full moon. Her wide, dark eyes were full of gratitude.

A soft, delighted laugh went through the company of soldiers. The leader of the soldiers came forward and introduced himself with great gentlemanliness. Soon Ae bowed and her heart beat a deep "Thank You" to Heavenly Father.

"You must have had a difficult time—and with such a cute little child along, too," commented the leader.

Soon Ae was not one to complain. She merely bowed her head again and thanked God once more, this time for the bravery and kindness of these defenders of Korea's freedom.

It was a thankful time for the soldiers, too. It always touched them to see the desperation and fear of the refugees—their brothers and sisters from the North. It reminded them of what they were here for. The little girl—that innocent face, that sweet little singing voice, those eyes full of trust and gratitude that said, "I just knew you'd rescue us!" made them chuckle and remember daughters and nieces and sisters at home. They were standing guard for their sake, too, against the aggressive new regime in the North.

These men were very kind to them. They welcomed them to the South and did everything they could to make them prepared for their further journey to Seoul, the capital of South Korea. They even gave them money to see them through.

"Seoul!" thought Soon Ae, as they waved their last goodbyes to the kind soldiers. "Surely we'll find the Messiah there." And she turned her face hopefully toward the great city.

True Mother singing when she was a child stopped the soldiers from firing their guns. Her beautiful little heart touched the communists in the North and the soldiers in the South and helped protect the three on their dangerous journey to freedom.

Refugees

Linna Rapkins

Three figures were on the road to the city. Every so often, they stopped, put the backs of their hands to their foreheads, and bowed all the way down to the ground three times. Then they walked on.

The city was Korea's capital, Seoul. The year was 1948, and the three figures were Mrs. Hong, her mother, and her six year old daughter, Hak Ja Han. Although they had been walking many days since escaping from the prison in Pyongyang, the girl was in good spirits, and her eyes sparkled with interest as the city came into view.

It wasn't a tall city with skyscrapers. Rather, all the buildings were less than five stories tall so they wouldn't stand taller than the Emperor's palace, which had for some decades now, stood without an emperor. Most of the people traveled by foot or bicycle. As the end of their journey came into view, Soon Ae Hong felt hopeful. Her brother might be here. Maybe—just maybe—a warm room awaited them.

She looked down at her daughter. "Such a good girl," she thought. "Never complaining, always optimistic and obedient. It's a sad thing, though, that her father never tried to work things out after she was born."

She glanced at her mother walking beside her. "Of course, Omma was pretty tough on him, telling him to be adopted into our family and then making a big fuss when he wanted to take his daughter to live somewhere else. His pride was hurt." She sighed. "Well, at least I don't think about him much anymore." Another sigh. "Still, I sure could use some manly support sometimes." For a woman alone to care for a child in Korea at that time was not easy.

Soon Ae remembered the home they had left behind: the dirt roads of the village, the cottage with the thatched roof, the persimmon tree—those things they would see no more. She thought also of the Inside Belly Church—gone forever. Mrs. Ho Ho Bin had refused to tell the police that she had not received revelations, even though she had received a note from a man in another cell telling her to deny everything. That man had told her to pray who had written the note so she could know the message was from heaven, but she didn't listen. She disobeyed the man (it was Sun Myung Moon) and she never came back from jail.

Another woman became the leader of the group. There had been a short but unforgettable conversation between Soon Ae and this woman.

"Who is this girl?" the woman had asked when she saw Soon Ae's daughter.

"This is my daughter, Hak ja Han," she had answered.

"How old is she?

"Six years old."

Then simply, but with quiet authority, she had said, "She will be the bride of the Lord!"

Just thinking about it gave Soon Ae that light-headed feeling that came whenever something unusual happened regarding her daughter, and she renewed her promise to God to take good care of her. That was her mission in life, it seemed. When they had been put into prison, she didn't know what to think. Should she stay calm, knowing that God was caring for her daughter? Or should she fight desperately to save her? In the end, she did both, and after eleven days, they escaped.

"Omma! Omma!" Hak Ja was tugging at her sleeve to get her attention.

"Yes, darling?"

"Will we be in Seoul today?"

"Yes, we will, daughter," she answered. "And don't forget that we will meet the Messiah very soon."

She looked at her mother to include her in this statement. "As we enter Seoul, we must remember to have the feeling that we are approaching him. We will continue to do our three bows regularly until we come to the edge of the city."

"Yes, Omma."

Mrs. Hong's own mother just looked at her wearily and nodded her head. By the afternoon, they were in the city, but still they continued walking.

"This city is endless," Soon Ae murmured with a worried look. "It could take days to find my brother." Her mother looked worried, too. It had been many years since she had seen her son, her only other child besides Soon Ae. Would they recognize him?

"We could pray, Omma," suggested her daughter.

"That we could, daughter," she agreed.

Soon Ae silently prayed for guidance as they walked. With the money the soldiers had given them at the border, they stopped at an outdoor counter and had some hot fish and noodle soup, and she continued her inner prayer.

As they got up to continue their journey among the street vendors, Soon Ae suddenly saw a familiar face. It was a friend of her brother—and an answer to her prayers. When she told him she was looking for her brother, he was very enthusiastic.

"Yes, he is here! He's a soldier and is stationed in Seoul now." He shook his head in disbelief. "He's been talking about his family a lot lately and wishing he could go home after all these years. And now here you are! Well, then, come along. I will take you to his place."

Before long, the reunited family was settled in Seoul. Hak Ja Han attended a nearby school, and Soon Ae worked to support her family.

During their first year in Seoul, the communists of North Korea were becoming a real threat. They made life miserable for the South whenever they possibly could. For example, the electricity would suddenly go off all over Seoul. That was because the electrical power came from the communists, who were fond of turning it off so the factories would have to close. Then they accused the southern Koreans of being lazy because their factories were closed.

By 1950, the North Korean communists, with supplies from Russia, began making attacks on the villages and moving closer to Seoul. The Americans were urgently called to help. The air became thick with tension during the sweltering heat of June and July. Koreans were leaving Seoul by the thousands, heading south to get far away from the hated communists.

Soon Ae and her mother and brother tried not to let Hak Ja Han see that they were worried. After she fell asleep each night, the adults discussed what to do. Things were getting scary. Perhaps the North Koreans would attack Seoul. Perhaps the Americans and the Russian communists would fight each other on their land and they would be caught in the middle. Should they flee? Then one day, Mrs. Hong's brother burst into the house all out of breath.

"Pack whatever you can in ten minutes," he said. "The families of soldiers are allowed to leave the city by train, and there's one leaving soon. Kapshida! Ppal-li, ppal-li!" ("Let's go! Quickly, quickly!")

They rushed around, tying bundles of their belongs onto their backs. It was difficult to run to the train on such a hot day, especially being loaded down as they were, but they managed to arrive before the train left.

The old train pulled slowly out of the station and chugged along—through the city, into the country, between the layered rice paddies, over a long bridge, and into the village of Kanko. They began to relax.

Through the open windows, they saw army jeeps and American soldiers weaving among the fleeing Koreans. These big soldiers appeared to be suffering greatly from the heat and were constantly slapping at the flies and insects which tormented them. They were also scratching a lot, so they probably had lice as well. Along the railroad tracks were thousands of people—mostly women, children, and old men in tall black hats—trudging south by foot. The few younger men were bent over double, barely able to hold up the massive bundles tied onto crude A-frames on their backs.

Suddenly: Pow! Bang! Crash! Crash! What was happening? Everyone stuck their heads out of the windows. Behind the train, they saw heavy black smoke billowing into the sky and below it, a gaping hole in the bridge they had been crossing upon five minutes before. If they had been just a few minutes late...they pulled their heads back inside, not wanting to think about that possibility.

Soon Ae closed her eyes. "God in heaven," she breathed shakily. "Thank you. I truly know that you are protecting my daughter—Your daughter."

They learned eventually that the American soldiers had destroyed the bridge in an attempt to stop the communists from going further south.

The Korean War had begun. Soon Ae and her daughter and mother arrived in the city of Taegu, where they decided to stay. Now, however, they could hear the guns of war, for the communists from the North had followed close behind. The blown-up bridges had not stopped them for long, and now they were fighting for Taegu. After that came Pusan, and then all of Korea would be theirs.

"Should we go on to Pusan?" wondered Soon Ae. She decided they would stay, and while the war raged around them like a big tornado, the three ladies concentrated on their daily lives. Hak Ja Han attended fifth grade. Always, they felt protected.

From time to time, God sent a reminder to Soon Ae to raise her daughter well. A monk once said to her, "You could never exchange this one daughter for even ten sons. This daughter is so honorable, she cannot touch the ground." (In Korea, if you are high class, they say your feet can't touch the ground.)

"Furthermore," he said, "your daughter will marry when she is very young, and she will marry an older man, a very wonderful, rich man. Money will come to him from the sky, from the land, and from the ocean."

Another time, as she was dropping off to sleep, Soon Ae heard a voice.

"Soon Ae," it said.

"I'm listening," she said in her mind.

"I want you to understand that your daughter must stay pure. She must not have any boyfriends. This is very, very important and your only mission is to protect her during the next few years."

"Thank you," said Mrs. Hong. "I understand."

She was already aware that some of her daughter's friends were boys, but they just seemed like brothers, so she hadn't been worried. However, Soon Ae had noticed that when they walked down the street together, older boys would often stare admiringly at her daughter. Some times they would boldly say something to her. "Mmm, beautiful!" Things like that.

She looked at her daughter. Her eyes were bright, her smile was beautiful, and she was pleasingly shy. There was a soft calmness about her face. She was only a child but she was blooming like a flower. No wonder the boys were looking at her.

"Hak Ja ya," her mother said, puttting her arm around her shoulders. "Do you know that you must not love any boy?"

"Yes, I understand, Omma," she answered promptly, as if she had already thought about it. But did she really understand? Soon Ae could only worry.

One day, a letter came to their house addressed to Hak Ja Han. When she opened it, her face reddened, and she tried to hide it.

"What's that?" her mother asked. Hak Ja Han handed the letter to her. As Soon Ae read it, her heart froze. It was from a boy, and he wrote, "Dear Hak Ja, I think you are beautiful. I love you very much."

"Do you know this boy?" asked her mother, trying to sound calm.

"He's just one of the boys at school," she answered.

"Well, daughter, please don't talk to him. Do you promise?"

"I promise, Omma," she said. She really wanted to do what was right. Unknown to her mother, she was already praying to be pure and to live for God. She even prayed for a pure husband.

In the days ahead, more things like this happened—more remarks on the street, more visitors, more letters. Soon Ae worried day and night.

"If it's like this now," she wondered, "what will happen when she is 13—or 16 years old?"

She thought about it. She prayed about it. An idea started coming into her head, but at first she dismissed it. It was too crazy. As she prayed, however, it became more clear. They must go away. They must live alone. She must give up everything to protect her daughter.

Soon Ae had to fear the war and many physical difficulties. Yet, even as a refugee, she thought of the Messiah and how to protect her daughter from sin.

Journey to Pusan

Renee Balise

"Escape to the south! Escape to the south!" This was everyone's goal. The war was all around them, and the communists were on the move. The safest place in Korea was as far south as anyone could get. Thousands of people set out every day for Pusan, at the southernmost tip of Korea. The roads were full of frightened people.

Sun Myung Moon, however, did not go south right away. He walked to Pyongyang from Hung Nam. It took him ten days. He wanted to check on his disciples in Pyongyang. Had they gone south? Were they safe? You don't leave people you consider your own family behind, and Sun Myung Moon had to show God and Satan that he loved these people juast as much as he loved his own family. Only in that way could all men and women come to be brothers and sisters.

Sun Myung Moon stayed in dangerous Pyongyang for 40 days, searching for his lost disciples. In the end, there was no time to go back to his own hometown. He never saw his parents again or many members of his family and it would be many decades before he got to go home. Like so many people in Korea in those times, they were lost in the storm of the war.

In Pyongyang, he found one disciple, Won Pil Kim. Together they went to visit each remaining disciple. To Sun Myung Moon's

Journey to Pusan

great disappointment, many of them had not remained steadfast. While he had been suffering so terribly in prison, they had become discouraged and gone back to living for themselves. Still, he went to see each one of them three times.

During this time, the war continued between the communists and the United Nations troops. The communists were led by two men. One was a Chinese man named Mao Tse-tung, and the other was a Korean named Kim Il Sung. Satan was using these two men to build the satanic kingdom on earth. God was using Sun Myung Moon to build the heavenly kingdom on earth.

Sun Myung Moon decided that he should go back once more to the southern part of Korea with the last two remaining disciples: Won Pil Kim and Mr. Jung Hwa Pak. Sun Myung Moon told Won Pil Kim, "You and Mr. Pak should prepare to go to the south with me right away."

Mr. Kim went to find Mr. Pak. They were hard and dangerous times and Mr. Pak had run into misfortune. His leg was broken.

"Teacher," Mr. Kim reported. "Mr. Pak has a broken leg and cannot walk. He has a big cast from the top of his leg all the way to the bottom. I found him lying down and feeling very sad because he thought you and I had already gone south without him."

Sun Myung Moon answered, "We are all going south together."

When Mr. Pak heard this news, he was so surprised. He cried and cried from happiness because Teacher Moon cared so much about him. It is not easy to find a true friend even when times are easy, but to find a true friend like Sun Myung Moon during war time was an incredible blessing!

They found an old bicycle at the house of Mr. Pak's sister. Sun Myung Moon struggled to put Mr. Pak on it. On December 4, 1950, in the middle of a very icy, cold winter, the three men, one teetering on an old bicycle, began their long, hard journey to Pusan in South

Korea. Sun Myung Moon pulled the bicycle from the front, and Won Pil Kim, who carried their packages, helped push from behind.

It was a most difficult and dangerous journey. They could not use the main roads because those roads were reserved for the United Nations troops. The middle roads were very crowded with people running away from the communists in the north. They had to use the smallest back roads, which led through dark woods, cold rivers, and steep mountains. Imagine trying to pull a person as big as yourself on a bicycle over mountains, through rivers and through the woods! Mr. Kim was amazed at Teacher Moon's strength, even after two and a half years in prison. He was even more amazed by his strong spirit. Sun Myung Moon was determined that they would make it to the south together—or they would not make it at all.

Sometimes the communists would shoot at the people from airplanes high in the sky. When the people saw this, they would run and try to save themselves, forgetting everyone else out of fear for their own lives. Sun Myung Moon never acted this way. No matter what happened, he always tried to protect Mr. Pak and Mr. Kim.

But it was back-breaking and heart-breaking hard work. Eventually, the poor man with the broken leg got so discouraged, he wanted to give up. He said, "Teacher, I just can't go on anymore. I am going to die anyway, so please go on without me."

"No!" Sun Myung Moon said. "That's no way to talk! How could you say such a thing? We pledged to God to live together and die together. You must not say such things!" He would not abandon him.

After many days, the three struggling men came to a province called Hwanghae Do. Two miles from there was an island named Yongmae. They heard that if they went there they could take a boat the rest of the way to Pusan. This would be much easier than walking. There was only one problem: how would they get to the island?

It was surrounded for two miles by water.

"What will I do now?" Mr. Pak moaned in pain. "I can't walk through the water for two miles with a broken leg!"

Sun Myung Moon told him, "I will get you there."

"How can you do that?" Mr. Pak asked doubtfully. "You cannot pull a bicycle through the ocean."

"When the tide goes out, I will put you on my back and carry you."

Mr. Pak was amazed. He wondered if Teacher Moon could really do it. Sure enough, when the tide went out, Sun Myung Moon put Mr. Pak on his back and began the walk through the cold, muddy, slippery ocean bottom. With each step, the mud clung to his feet, making them very heavy.

While he walked, he gained the strength to carry Mr. Pak by thinking and praying, "This man represents all the people of the world. If I cannot succeed in carrying him to this island, then my mission to save the world cannot succeed." In spite of years of hunger and mistreatment in prison and the current pain and fear, Sun Myung Moon carried Mr. Pak across the water.

Finally, the three of them did make it to the island. Sun Myung Moon was so tired he was panting. A boat was just leaving for the south, but there were more people than could possibly fit on the boat. They realized they couldn't get on. Sun Myung Moon saw people thinking only of saving themselves, and he felt deep pain and sadness to see people acting that way. How miserable they were!

He turned to his companions. Sadly, he said, "We must go back."

The boat left. It was hopeless to think about going South on a boat now. Sun Myung Moon knew they must leave before the communists came, so once again, when the tide went out, he put Mr. Pak on his back and carried him the two miles back to Hwanghae Do. Again, they walked slowly through the thick, heavy mud.

When they arrived back on land, his first thought was for the two men. He prayed, "Heavenly Father, even if I must sacrifice, it is all right as long as my brothers are given something to comfort them and give them hope."

Heavenly Father promised them, "Tonight someone will feed you well."

They began to walk. Sun Myung Moon's hair was cut in the prison style and a policemen who saw them thought he was a communist. He struck Sun Myung Moon a blow on the head. They explained to the policeman that Sun Myung Moon was a minister returning from prison. He expertly quoted the Bible, and the policeman then believed them and let them go. Sun Myung Moon prayed that God could accept this sacrifice for the sake of his brothers' comfort.

Soon it was night. The three men walked in complete darkness, trying to head south. On and on they trudged—so tired, so dirty, so hungry.

Suddenly they saw a light sparkling in the distance! As they went toward the light, they saw it was a house. Mr. Pak and Mr. Kim were filled with joy. When Sun Myung Moon knocked on the door, it was answered by a young schoolteacher and his wife. They had been preparing to go south but hadn't left yet.

"My name is Moon Sun Myung and these are my friends, Kim Won Pil and Jung Hwa Pak," said Sun Myung Moon, in the fashion of Korean culture. He told him about all their experiences and the man felt sorry for their sufferings.

"You are very welcome here," the schoolteacher said. "Your road has been very hard. I don't have much, but what I have I will gladly share with you."

He fed them a nice dinner and invited them to sleep in the warmest part of the house where he and his wife usually slept. The next

Journey to Pusan

morning, he killed a chicken and made them a wonderful breakfast. Sun Myung Moon was so grateful to God for this wonderful gift. It had come because he had been willing to suffer for his friends.

Soon they set out to complete the journey. By the end of December, 1950, the three men reached Seoul in South Korea. Many of the houses were already deserted, because the communists were coming. It was almost like a ghost town. Sun Myung Moon decided they should continue on their way to Pusan, which was at the southern tip of Korea. Mile after long mile, they walked. Sometimes wonderful things would happen. Once they came to a town where they had all the apples they could eat! In another town, they were given all the rice cakes they could eat.

Mr. Pak's broken leg finally healed, and the cast could be taken off. Then they came to a place named Kyung Ju City and Mr. Pak, worn out by the long journey, begged to stay there, where he had relatives. Sun Myung Moon that this would be the best thing and agreed.

Then he and Mr. Kim went on to another town called Ulsan. There they were able to catch a train to Pusan. It was a cargo train, and there wasn't any room for them to sit, so they had to hang on to the front where the engine was running and the coal was burning. Sun Myung Moon's clothes became black with grease and dirt from the train but it was much faster than walking.

On January 27, 1951, about two months after they began their journey, they reached the area of Choyang Young Station in Pusan, where they would begin a new life.

Even under desperate circumstances, True Father put his friends ahead of himself and willingly sacrificed himself so that they could have an easier time.

Life in Pusan

Linna Rapkins

The calendars said January 27, 1951. The old train rattled to a stop at Pusan station. The two young men who climbed stiffly down from the front of the train were so blackened by soot and dirt, and so frozen by the January wind, that even their own parents could not have recognized them.

For two long months, they had been crawling over snowy mountains, carrying a man with a broken leg. They'd trudged through rocky valleys and icy waters. For two long months, they had been eating roots from the ground and buying small servings of rice whenever someone gave them a little money. For two endless months, they had been sleeping on frozen ground without a warm blanket or coat. They had pushed themselves to their limits—and then they had pushed some more.

They peered out into the darkness; then looked at each other and smiled. Their smiles said, "Pusan, at last!" But their weary bodies cried out to them, "A little rest, please! Some sleep!"

They looked all around the cold train station and found an old butter can left by the United Nations soldiers. In this, they made a fire and soon received a little warmth. Although they felt as if they were still rocking and bumping with the train, they soon fell into an exhausted sleep.

As soon as the morning sky began to lighten, Sun Myung Moon and his beloved disciple, Won Pil Kim, woke up and wasted no time in venturing out into the chilled, gray streets of Pusan. On three sides, they could just make out a city that seemed to wrap itself around the steep hills. On the remaining side was a body of water. Pusan was a port city and ships were being loaded and unloaded even at this early hour.

Sun Myung Moon's first thought was, "How can I quickly find those who worked with me in Seoul and Pyongyang? Heavenly Parent, You have been crying for them. I must find them quickly, quickly!"

As they pushed their tired bodies along, he thought of the separation from his followers while in prison. He thought about his search for them in Pyongyang afterwards and his heartbreaking disappointment when he found so few. He thought about the possibility of finding them in Pusan, and new strength came to him.

Sun Myung Moon and Won Pil Kim spent their first day walking the streets and looking hopefully into the thousands of faces. With the little money they had left, they bought a small snack, which was their meal for the day. It didn't give them much energy for climbing up and down the steep hills, but they kept climbing anyway.

Pusan was the only city in all Korea where no Chinese soldiers swarmed through the streets. It was crowded with thousands and thousands of people who had left their homes in the North to escape the threats of the communist soldiers. If they were very lucky, they had moved in with relatives or friends in Pusan. If they were a somewhat lucky, they were living in tents outside the city. Others slept in corners, gateways, or any small space they could find. Since Sun Myung Moon and Won Pil Kim were among the last refugees to arrive in Pusan, every spot seemed to be taken.

They soon found someone Sun Myung Moon had taught in Seoul about five years earlier. They were invited to spend the night in his house. What a treat to sleep in an actual room and eat some steaming rice! It wasn't the white, clean rice we eat today. It was hard and gritty and mixed with barley, but it was all that was available to most Koreans during those difficult war years.

Sun Myung Moon looked around at the crowded room. He didn't want to cause more hardship for these already suffering people, so the next day he insisted on leaving.

Won Pil Kim thought to himself, "Because there are two of us, it will be very difficult for people to invite us in. I must find a way to take care of myself, so it will be easier for Teacher Moon to find a place to stay." He told Teacher Moon what he wanted to do, and soon he found a job in a restaurant with a place to sleep nearby.

That same day, Sun Myung Moon noticed a man in the street staring at him. He was looking at Sun Myung Moon's ragged, dirty clothes and rubber shoes and thinking, "Who is that man? He looks familiar. But I don't know any beggars." Then his eyes lit up in recognition.

"Moon!" he cried excitedly as he came up to Sun Myung Moon. Then Sun Myung Moon recognized his schoolmate, Duk Moon Aum. They had gone to the university in Japan together years before. They laughed and embraced with joy.

Mr. Aum immediately invited Sun Myung Moon to his home. He had become a professor and architect, yet he lived with his family in only a small apartment. There was hardly any heat, and the food was simple, but at least it was a place to get out of the cold wind, and Sun Myung Moon was grateful.

Instead of relaxing, however, Sun Myung Moon immediately began talking to Mr. Aum about the ideal world and about Jesus. Mr. Aum was a Buddhist, so he didn't know much about Jesus.

That night he had a surprising dream. In this dream, Jesus' sister spoke to him.

"When Jesus was alive," she said, "his mother—our mother—didn't understand him. She kept fussing at him to stay home and become a good carpenter. Now in spirit world, Jesus feels resentment toward her. It might have been possible for him to succeed if his mother had prepared him and supported him as the Messiah. The only person who can help Jesus now is your friend, Sun Myung Moon. Please listen to him and help him!"

The next morning Mr. Aum told Sun Myung Moon his dream.

Sun Myung Moon responded, "I have many things to explain to you."

They sat in Mr. Aum's little home, and Sun Myung Moon told him all about the ideal world, the Fall, Jesus' mission, and God's heart. When Mr. Aum heard the wise words of Sun Myung Moon, he came to understand that his old school mate was very special. Even though they had been just friends before, he began calling Sun Myung Moon "Sonsaeng nim" (Honorable Teacher).

After about a week, Sun Myung Moon told Mr. Aum he had to go visit some other people. Actually, he had no place to go, but he saw how crowded it was for Mr. Aum's family, and he didn't want to be a burden.

As he walked through the streets, Sun Myung Moon prayed earnestly. It was a miracle that among the thousands of people he met, he quickly found another friend from his earlier days. It was Mr. Kim who had been in Hung Nam prison. He was the one who had followed Sun Myung Moon's advice about working in an easier part of the prison and escaping when something looked suspicious. They were overjoyed to see each other.

"I've been wishing all this time I could report to you," said Mr. Kim excitedly. "I followed your advice in prison, and when the communists started killing prisoners, I was able to escape. At last, I have the opportunity to thank you for my life."

Sun Myung Moon looked at him with a big smile.

"As you can see, I eventually made it to Pusan. I got a job, and now I'm happy to tell you I just got married. Will you please come to my house and meet my bride? We would be most honored to have you stay with us."

Sun Myung Moon agreed to go. When they arrived, he saw that Mr. Kim indeed had a nice wife, but he saw also that they had only one small room. He stayed two weeks so he could talk to his friend about Heavenly Parent's plan for Korea and the world, but he understood how difficult it was for the newly married couple to have another man living in the same room with them. Again, he moved on.

Sun Myung Moon's desire was to find more of his followers. However, he had to get a job in order to survive. He found work at the docks, where he spent his precious time loading and unloading ships. It was backbreaking work, and he was still in a weakened condition from prison life and the long trip to Pusan. Although spring was just around the corner, the icy winds still whistled through this port city.

Sun Myung Moon learned that if he worked during the night when it was coldest, it helped to keep him warm. Then he could sleep during the day when it was warmer. Sometimes he would sleep under someone's porch, but often he would climb one of the mountains, where he could pray and sleep undisturbed.

He also continued to visit Mr. Aum and Mr. Kim, and often he went to see how Won Pil Kim was doing at the restaurant. One day, he brought Mr. Aum and Mr. Kim along to the restaurant.

Won Pil Kim went to his boss and asked, "May I offer this man and his guests some food? He is my honorable teacher."

Life in Pusan

"Alright," said the understanding owner. "They can use the private room in the back, and you may serve them rice and a few things."

Won Pil Kim eagerly pressed the rice down tightly into the bowls so he could pile more on top. He felt so much joy to be able to serve. Sun Myung Moon thanked him cheerfully and asked how he was doing.

"I'm doing well," answered Won Pil Kim. It seemed like only a moment and Sun Myung Moon's rice was all eaten. Won Pil Kim refilled the bowl, and again the rice was eaten almost immediately. Then he understood that even though Sun Myung Moon looked happy and well and didn't ask for anything, he was actually starving.

"Why didn't he tell me he was so hungry?" wondered Won Pil Kim. "Why didn't he ask for something special? He just accepts whatever I set before him." Then he promised himself, "I will make sure to prepare plenty of food for him whenever he comes." And he always did.

They had been in Pusan almost four months. In May, Sun Myung Moon found a cheap room in a boarding house for homeless workers.

He came to Won Pil Kim and suggested, "We could rent a room together at this boarding house. Then we could be together again and save money as well. How does that sound?"

"It sounds wonderful," said Won Pil Kim enthusiastically, for he missed being with his beloved teacher so very much.

When they moved in, they found that the room was more like a closet. They couldn't even stretch out full length to sleep. Later, when Mr. Aum sometimes spent the night with them, he had to sleep leaning against the wall. But they didn't care. It was a great comfort to be together again.

As time went on, Won Pil Kim came to appreciate much more deeply the greatness of Sun Myung Moon. He saw how he was always thinking of others. He saw that Sun Myung Moon never complained about the cold that chilled his bones day and night. He never mentioned the prison wounds that still caused him pain. He never mentioned the pangs of hunger in his shrunken stomach. He never said, "Oh, I wish I could taste some bulgoki and fresh kimchi and some really good quality white rice."

Instead, he would look kindly at Won Pil Kim and ask, "Are you alright? Did you get something to eat today? Are you warm enough?"

Won Pil Kim always reassured him he was fine. But actually, he was hungry and tired most of the time. Neither one wanted to worry the other—so great was their love.

The pain in True Father's heart during those painful early times in his ministry was greater than the pain in his body when he looked at his young, faithful disciple. "I'm sorry you must suffer so much," he would say silently. "You gave up everything. Now you are in rags, and your stomach cries out constantly for food." Father's tears would flow for this dear young man who had come so many miles with him.

True Father was this kind of person. When we suffered, he suffered. Perhaps we can still say to him, "It's alright, Father. Don't worry about me. I want to help you. I want to be your disciple."

Then his eyes, looking upon from the spiritual world, will fill with tears, and he will feel better. And God's eyes will fill with tears, and God, too, will feel better.

Even without food or a place to live in, like a true parent, True Father's first concern was for the welfare of others.

Part 3

The Early Days of the Unification Movement

A House Built On Rock

Linna Rapkins

"We must get a place of our own," said Sun Myung Moon one hot summer night. "We have been in Pusan for almost six months now. If we continue living in this tiny room, we will never be able to invite guests and have space to teach.

Won Pil Kim nodded his head in agreement but without much feeling of hope. As he wiped the sweat from his brow, he thought to himself, "Where will we ever get enough money for a place of our own? And where will we even find a place? Every dwelling in all Pusan is surely full to overflowing."

Sun Myung Moon didn't seem to notice the heat. His brow formed a thoughtful wrinkle.

"I want to show you a place tomorrow, Won Pil."

The next morning, Won Pil Kim followed Sun Myung Moon up the steep Pom Net Kol hill where Sun Myung Moon spent many hours meditating and praying. They climbed beyond the city to a place where only a cemetery and one house stood.

"The Pusan people tell a story," said Sun Myung Moon, "that on this hill, a white tiger once appeared. For that reason, no one wants to live here. They are so superstitious.

"We will build a house right here," he announced as he pointed to a huge rock rising out of the rough, rocky ground. He did not look at his young disciple's surprised face but continued sharing his plans enthusiastically. "We will gather stones and wood and anything else we can find for our building. But first, we must level this spot off. I already found a shovel and a sack. We can fill it with dirt from over there, dump it here, and pack it down tight. That will be our floor."

He had already picked up an old shovel and a big cloth bag from their hiding place and was walking to the place he had pointed out. Won Pil Kim followed him and soon found himself holding the bag while Sun Myung Moon shoveled dirt into it. When it was full, Won Pil Kim carried it near the big rock and dumped it into the holes. By the time he returned, Sun Myung Moon had more dirt already dug up to shovel into the bag. After awhile, they changed jobs. Sun Myung Moon worked so fast, however, Won Pil Kim couldn't get very much dirt dug up before Sun Myung Moon was back for another load.

All through the month of August, they went to their jobs. They visited people. They prayed. Then they climbed the long hill in the summer heat and worked on their little house. For many weeks, they could only build it on Sundays when they were off from work.

Sun Myung Moon and Won Pil Kim gathered stones from everywhere. They carried them a few at a time to the chosen spot and piled them carefully on top of each other. They stuck smaller rocks and handfuls of soil in between the rocks to hold them in place. The rocks formed the lower part of the house. The upper part was made mostly of wooden boxes, but in some cases, they even used cardboard boxes. They knew that when it rained, these boxes wouldn't last very long, but there weren't enough wooden boxes to be found.

Twice, as they were building, the house fell down, but Sun Myung Moon never even frowned. He just figured out what was wrong and began again. Finally, on the third try, it grew into something resembling a house—a shack, really. On clear nights, Sun Myung Moon and Won Pil Kim would be able to admire the stars through the cracks in their roof. In wet weather, rain would drip through and turn their dirt floor into mud. But they were so eager to move in!

One day in September, they were able to stand back and admire their finished handiwork. Their very own home! Here they would be able to stretch out to sleep. They would be free from the landlord's questioning eyes. They could cook their own meals. They could breathe fresh air.

And most of all, they could invite people in whenever they wished—for this house was not just for themselves. It was for doing God's work.

Before they even thought of moving their few belongings in, they knelt down to pray. They thanked God for their new home and dedicated it to God. This humble hut of boxes and stones was accepted by our Heavenly Parent as God's most holy house.

Soon they moved into the little stone and cardboard shack by the spring on the hill. There were no closets, no kitchen, no bathroom—just one room large enough for two people to stretch out, with some space at one end for their things.

They found a piece of canvas to put over the dirt floor. This would be their carpet and bed. A flimsy wooden box used for shipping oranges—called an orange crate—was pulled out during the day to serve as the table. There was an old kerosene lamp to light up the nights.

Just a few steps away was a little spring of water.

"Tomorrow we will dig the dirt out of that little spring so the water can come up more freely," said Sun Myung Moon to Won Pil Kim. "But tonight we sit down and give thanks and enjoy."

Sun Myung Moon's friend from his student days, Duk Moon Aum, came to the new home, and they had a celebration. They cooked their dinner of rice over an open fire outside the hut. As before, the only kind of rice they could get was old and was mixed with little stones that stuck in their teeth when they ate it. That kind of rice would be thrown out or given to animals today, but they were grateful to have even that. Sun Myung Moon washed it carefully by the spring and got the little stones out. He cooked it over the fire. He had learned how to cook rice so the top part was cooked without burning the bottom part. Ask anyone today if she can cook a perfect pot of rice over an open fire, and she will say, "No! I cannot do that. I need a stove or rice cooker." It is very difficult.

They ate outside, overlooking the other hills and the city below. As the sun disappeared for the night, Sun Myung Moon turned to Mr. Aum.

"Duk Moon-Ah, please sing a song for us."

Mr. Aum sang a Korean folk song. It sounded so wonderful, Sun Myung Moon urged him to sing some more. As would happen many times in the days and nights to come, Mr. Aum sang for hours—Korean songs, Italian folk songs, opera songs, many kinds of songs. His voice was strong and carried over the hills of Pusan as a kind of blessing.

Sun Myung Moon sat quietly watching the lights flickering on in the city below. His mind seemed to be far away, close by, everywhere all at once. He seemed to be thinking of the past, the present and the future. The music and the night blended together with the thoughts of this special man who would become our True Father.

Sometime after midnight, the three men said one more prayer and went into the little house to sleep. Even though it felt like a palace compared to what they had before, it was actually very small. With three adults, it was crowded. Sun Myung Moon and Mr. Aum slept on each side by the walls, and Won Pil Kim, the youngest of the three, slept in the middle with his head down by their feet and his feet up by their heads.

The stars twinkled down on them through the cracks in the roof. The September breezes blew in on them. The hills seemed to echo the songs of Mr. Aum and add new notes of comfort and joy. The little spring bubbled happily and the trees stretched their boughs out protectively over this holy ground.

Each morning, Sun Myung Moon woke up before the sun. In the darkness, he would climb farther up the Pom Net Kol mountain for meditation and prayer. He had received so much through revelation, but there was still much more to learn. He had to spend time praying to learn these things and make plans for the months and years ahead. As always, he spent many hours just being with Heavenly Parent, comforting and loving God.

Sun Myung Moon's favorite spot was a rocky place that stuck out from the hillside like a little cliff. Behind him was the woodsy area of the mountain as it continued higher. Before him were the valleys and hills of Pusan. He looked out from this point each day until he knew by heart every curve and dip of the other hills against the sky. He paid no attention to the cold, hard rock beneath him.

As he poured out his heart to Heavenly Parent, he repented again and again for all the pain that had been brought to God over the centuries. He repented for the churches who had not united with him. He repented for those who had left him.

Another person might have said, "Heavenly Father, I have already prayed many hours for the world. I have endured pain in prison. I have cried many hours for the world and for You. I cannot cry for you anymore. It's time to get a little rest."

Sun Myung Moon didn't think that way. Again and again, as he prayed for each part of history, he sobbed with grief as he felt the agony and loneliness of God. Just as he had done when he was younger, he cried until it seemed that there could be no tears left in him; yet the tears continued to pour like a torrent down his face and onto the rock beneath him. Morning after morning, this was his life.

In later years, among the many Blessed Families that were to come, the big flat rock where Sun Myung Moon usually prayed became known as the "Rock of Tears." It was washed by True Father's tears so many times, it must be the holiest rock in all the world.

When Sun Myung Moon climbed down from the mountain each day, he had many things to do. His mind was always far ahead of his body, planning what had to be done and how to do it. He walked quickly wherever he went, as if this were the most important moment in all history. If others were with him, they could hardly keep up with him.

He felt so impatient—impatient to get things done; impatient to find more people. So many years had passed, and he had only a few people with him in Pusan. He was already over 30 years old.

Now there was another urgent job to do. He must write down all of his revelations. Up to this point, Sun Myung Moon had been teaching the people himself. He read the stories directly from his well-worn Bible and explained to each person what the stories meant.

But he knew he couldn't continue forever teaching each person himself. It was important that he write everything down that had been revealed to him so that more people could learn about these stories and so that the details would not be forgotten. Soon God would bring him a person who could put these revelations into a book, and many people would come to hear God's words. Sun Myung Moon had to be prepared. Every moment was precious and urgent.

When Sun Myung Moon returned from his morning prayers, he immediately sat down to write. Many times, as Won Pil Kim left for work, Sun Myung Moon was already sitting by the orange crate writing furiously, trying to keep up with all the information that came to him from God. He learned to sharpen many pencils before starting so he could keep up with the words that came into his head. Some days, when Won Pil Kim, Duk Moon Aum, or someone else was there, their job was to sharpen the pencils with a little knife. Sun Myung Moon wrote so fast, the pencils wore down almost immediately, and they could not always keep enough sharpened for him. Sun Myung Moon's hand always got very tired. From time to time, he gave it a shake and then continued writing, even though it hurt.

When Won Pil Kim returned from work in the evening, he would often find Sun Myung Moon still writing at his little "desk." His eyes were red with weariness, his hand cramped into the writing position, his legs stiff from sitting on the floor all day. Often, he had forgotten to eat anything.

But as the days went by, the stack of finished pages grew. Sometimes ideas would come to Sun Myung Moon before he could get a sheet of paper, and he would quickly write them on the cardboard walls. Soon the walls and ceiling were covered with writing. Information was coming from heaven day and night, and it had to be written down before it was lost.

One night, Sun Myung Moon suddenly sat up and shook Won Pil Kim awake,

"Won Pil-A! Won Pil-A! Wake up! Light the lamp—Ppal-li, ppal-li!" ("Quickly, quickly!")

Won Pil Kim sat up with a jerk and quickly lit the old kerosene lamp. He looked with sleepy eyes at the pencil and paper Sun Myung Moon had set before him.

"Please write what I tell you," said Sun Myung Moon, without further explanation.

Won Pil Kim picked up the pencil and poised his hand over the paper. He gave his head a shake and rubbed his eyes with his other hand to get rid of the sleepiness.

Sun Myung Moon began to talk. Won Pil Kim's pencil moved up and down as fast as he could make it go as he tried to keep up with everything Sun Myung Moon said. Sun Myung Moon told all about the Lord of the Second Advent. He explained why such a man must come to earth, what he must do, where he will come, when he will come, everything. Sun Myung Moon didn't have to stop and think what to say next or rewrite any of it so it would sound better. The words came out of his mouth as if they were already written somewhere.

They were coming directly from Heavenly Parent.

Soon, Won Pil Kim's hand was throbbing with pain. Sun Myung Moon kept sharpening more pencils for him so he could continue writing without stopping. The words kept coming. Then it stopped just as suddenly as it had begun.

"Thank you," said Sun Myung Moon. "It is finished." He added these pages to the rest of the stack.

Won Pil Kim lay gratefully down on the canvas mat and closed his eyes. His hand still felt cramped as he fell asleep for the few minutes remaining before it was time to wake up again. The first Divine Principle had been written, and the last chapter was in his handwriting.

When morning dawned, Sun Myung Moon was already on the mountain, praying. Won Pil Kim got up to prepare for work, and as he ate his morning rice and thought over what had happened the night before, the day felt very special.

"I see it now!" he exclaimed to himself as he started down the hill. "Now I understand! Sun Myung Moon is the Lord of the Second Advent! He is the Second Coming of the Messiah. That's why he told me years ago that there would never be another group like this one. I've lived with him and worked with him all this time, and I never really understood until now." The events of the night kept going through his head.

"So that's how he gets his revelations!" he thought in awe. "It comes through him directly from God. He hears it in his head or sees it in his mind—or something! When he writes so furiously all day, that's what is happening to him. Now I see!"

Won Pil Kim reached the bottom of the mountain and picked his way through the bustling streets. He hardly noticed all the people on their way to work.

"If I hadn't done that writing for him last night, no one—no one—would ever have known how he receives his revelations. He had to let me learn it so I could explain to others!" He shook his head incredulously.

As he reached his place of work, he noticed for the first time the crowds of people around him.

"They have no idea," he thought, as he watched them scurrying about. "They think there's nothing more to life than work and food. A bowl of rice and a warm floor is all they ask. They don't know the Lord of the Second Advent is here—now—in Pusan!"

He felt like shouting the news to them, but just then he reached the door of his place of work. He paused.

"How can I do such meaningless work at a time like this? The Messiah is here. I would rather be doing his work, God's work." Should he go back up the hill? He thought it over a moment.

"No!" he answered himself. "I, out of all the people on this earth, can earn money today for the Lord of the Second Advent!"

Won Pil Kim slid the door open and stepped in. He would earn the money with all his heart today.

Because of True Father's heart, even a shack made of old cardboard boxes became a holy place filled with the beauty of God's love.

A Little Peace

Chris Garcia

Won Pil Kim sat at the long steel table in the army mess hall, finishing off a plate of potatoes and ham. It was a feast, but American food was so different than anything he had eaten before. It was hard to get used to. Still, he knew that ham and potatoes were a lot better than what most of his fellow Koreans were having for dinner right now.

Suddenly, he thought of his mother's taen jang jigae stew—and the summer-style kimchi with a steaming bowl of barley and clean white rice. He hardly ever thought of his family anymore, but today his thoughts wandered back to northern Korea, and he wondered if they were even alive. He didn't know, couldn't know. War had changed so many things. And his life with Sun Myung Moon had changed so many things. Anyway, he knew he had a lot to be thankful for. Every day, he came to the American army base and worked with Ju Won, another Korean refugee, painting buildings.

He wiped his hands on his gray coveralls. They were spotted with gobs of gray paint and gray fingerprints. He knew God had been good to him. And yet, he felt it wasn't so much because of him, but because of Sun Myung Moon that he had received so much blessing. With Won Pil Kim's job, they could buy the basics of survival, and

Sun Myung Moon could go on with his mission for God. That was most important.

Sun Myung Moon had also worked at the army base as a carpenter. It seemed that he could do just about any job he decided to do, even building things. During that time, Sun Myung Moon sometimes finished work first. Then he would come to where Won Pil Kim was working and wait for him so they could walk home together.

Won Pil Kim finished his meal with a cup of coffee. He was learning to like coffee a little. It had that bitter twang that the Korean soul naturally likes. All the Americans drank coffee. They made a big deal out of it. They wanted him to drink it black. "Like a man," was how they said it.

The army guys liked him because he was sweet-natured and sympathetic. He was friendly, never complained, and didn't have to have someone standing over him all the time to make sure he did things right.

"You're alright," they would say. He tried to learn the word. They also liked him because he never stole anything.

He got up and took his tin plate and cup over to the kitchen. He handed them to the Korean man washing the dishes. Behind this man, Won Pil Kim noticed a stack of pictures on a crate of onions.

"What are those?" he asked.

"Those are Ju Won's pictures," said the dishwasher man. "He left them here. And if you see him, can you tell him he better not leave them here anymore? They're going to get messed up."

Won Pil Kim went over to have a look. He picked up the stack of photos and thumbed through them. They were black and white photographs of soldiers and their families.

"Why does Ju Won have these?" he asked.

"I think he paints them or something," said the man. "I'm not sure."

"Does he get paid for it?" asked Won Pil Kim.

"Yeah. The soldiers like stuff like that."

"Interesting," said Won Pil Kim. Foreign faces from other countries. Most of them were probably Americans, he figured, although there were soldiers here from all over the world.

Now that the worst fighting was over and a truce had been called, most of the soldiers were going home—except for the Americans. Thank God for General Douglas MacArthur. The General and his men were like a wall holding back Kim II Sung and the North Korean Army.

"I'll take the pictures to Ju Won," offered Won Pil Kim. He headed for the tool shed. He found Ju Won washing some brushes with turpentine.

"You're working so hard," said Won Pil Kim.

"Not that hard," answered Ju Won politely. "Finished for the day?"

"Yes. I just brought you these." He held out the pictures.

Ju Won stopped washing brushes and looked up with a surprised look on his face. He pushed his thick glasses up on his nose and peered at Won Pil Kim.

In North Korea, this painter had been a rich and well-respected lawyer. People had come to him with complex problems, which he solved with his sharp mind. Now he was painting walls all day and cleaning paint brushes.

That's what war does to you sometimes, thought Won Pil Kim.

"Ah, yes! Thank you very much," answered Ju Won. Then he sighed, as he said, "I don't know how I'm ever going to finish all these tonight."

"What do you do with them? Do you think I could help?" asked Won Pil Kim.

"I'd be glad for you to help. I draw a picture from the photo, and then I paint it so it looks like a portrait," he explained. "You could help by painting some of it in after I draw it."

Won Pil Kim was pleased. Just a few days ago Sun Myung Moon had seen a sketch of his and had told him he should practice a little each day and develop his skills. What a coincidence!

The two young men found a spot and got to work on the pictures. Ju Won saw that Won Pil Kim did very well. He felt bad, though, that Won Pil Kim was doing such a nice thing for him without pay. Then he had an idea.

"Won Pil-A," he said. "I've got more pictures than I can handle right now. Let me give you one photo to do. Just sketch it and paint it in like I've been doing. Here's some paint and paper. I'll give you 10 won. What do you say?"

"Alright," said Won Pil Kim, using the only English word he knew. Ju Won laughed. "Alright."

It was getting dark outside as Won Pil Kim headed home. He stopped at the front gate of the army base where a soldier stepped out and stamped his passbook. Korean people looked at him enviously as he passed. He felt sorry for them, for all of them.

His thoughts went back to Pyongyang, the city where he had lived with his family and friends. This seemed to be a day for remembering. He had lived in a fairly nice house—nothing great, but always clean and comfortable. His family had lived there for generations—his parents, his grandparents, his great-grandparents. He smiled as he remembered his dear aunt, who had invited him to hear a man speak. Everything had changed for him then. He had become part of "The Weeping Church." It was called that because when Sun Myung Moon preached a sermon, he wept. And when he prayed, he wept. And when he began to weep, everybody in the group began to weep, too. So it was "The Weeping Church."

He trudged up the muddy hill, slipping here and there. Maybe someday people would want to hear about his experiences with

Sun Myung Moon. But when he imagined getting up in front of a congregation like the one they had had in Pyongyang, it seemed impossible! Finally, the little hut came into view—home!—and there at the door was Sun Myung Moon.

"Good evening, Won Pil-a," he called out with a smile.

"Good evening, " answered Won Pil Kim, his face brightening.

As he lifted the cardboard flap (their door) aside, part of it came off in his hand. Soon they would need to replace it.

The kerosene railroad lantern lit up the room with a warm, yellow light. There was a little charcoal grill off to the side, which they used to boil water and cook meals whenever they couldn't cook outside. Sometimes in the winter, they would wake up in the morning with a thin line of snow on their clothes where it had snowed in through the breaks in the roof.

"Look what I have," said Won Pil Kim, and he took out the photograph and the paints, brushes, and good paper. He found a dry spot on the floor and sat down. Sun Myung Moon took the photo and held it up to the lantern light for a better look.

"Where did you get this?" he asked.

"Ju Won gave it to me. If I can draw a picture from this photograph and paint it, he will pay me ten won. Isn't that a good idea?" Sun Myung Moon looked impressed. He examined the picture slowly, fascinated.

Won Pil Kim watched and waited. In the lantern light, he looked at Sun Myung Moon's face. It was thin and serious. It was the face of a man who had not had enough to eat, nor had much rest for many years. It was not the look of a starving or tired man, but the look of a man with much to do and much on his mind.

"Have you eaten today?" Won Pil Kim asked gently.

"No, I guess I haven't," said Sun Myung Moon, setting the photo down. "I fixed some food, but then I gave it to the people who came today. I taught them, and then I fed them. They had no money. The rest I used to buy matches. I'm so sorry the money is gone already. You worked so hard for it."

"It's alright," said Won Pil Kim, feeling a little uncomfortable that Sun Myung Moon was explaining so much to him. He didn't have to.

"I want you to know just how the money is spent," persisted Sun Myung Moon It was Sun Myung Moon's way of letting him know that he was very careful with the money Won Pil Kim earned, even though it seemed that they never had any. Won Pil Kim could not help but appreciate Sun Myung Moon's thoughtfulness.

Picking up the photo again, Won Pil Kim said, "I've never seen anyone like this, have you?" It was a black and white photo of a beautiful black girl with a rather flat nose and large lips. She had dark, very curly hair. "What color do you think I should paint her?"

Sun Myung Moon wasn't sure. He'd never seen such a person either.

"Maybe brown," he suggested. "Yes, brown is nice."

Won Pil Kim set to work on the picture. All the while Sun Myung Moon sat by his side, watching. For four hours, he worked. Finally, he finished and put the paints away.

As he lay down on the mat, Won Pil Kim gazed sleepily at the walls around him. He looked at the names on the boxes, which were all in English, and he wondered what they said. He had brought some of them from the army base and they were colored with advertisements for American food and drinks. Among these advertisements were the amazing things Sun Myung Moon had written in Chinese and Korean characters all over the boxes. Sometimes something would come to him while he was praying, sometimes he would jump out of his sleep with some new revelation, which he would quickly scribble on the wall in the dark, not taking the time to find pencil and paper.

Not many people had wallpaper like this!

Sun Myung Moon put out the lamp and the room was instantly dark. A soft breeze blew through a chink in the wall. Won Pil Kim put his hands under his head, feeling very tired and a bit lonely. Much as he loved Sun Myung Moon, living with him wasn't always easy. Sometimes he felt so little, his concerns so small. Sometimes Sun Myung Moon's ideas and dreams were just too big for him. Sometimes he wished he could be like a tree, like a rice field or a bamboo forest when the wind blows across the water, simple and at peace.

But sometimes God chooses you for something great whether you feel worthy of it or not. And that's an honor.

Outside, he could hear sounds of the night: the bark of a dog far down the hill, little night animals scurrying through the hills. He heard the squash, squash, squashing of footsteps coming up the hill, past the side of the shack to the little well Sun Myung Moon had dug. The sound of a bucket. The sound of water. The sound of some weary soul squash, squash, squashing away again.

Many people down the hill had heard about the little spring of clean water up by the shack where the two young men lived. They would come all the way up the steep hill just to fetch some of it, for clean water was hard to find in Pusan. Sun Myung Moon and Won Pil Kim were known to be polite young men, so people felt free to come.

Won Pil Kim listened for the sound he knew would soon come. There it was. Yes. Sun Myung Moon was praying. Sometimes the praying became singing. The singing was praying. And soon another sound would come. Yes, there it was, too. Sobbing. Desperate weeping. Won Pil Kim began to dream that he was back in the Weeping Church again, back in Pyongyang.

The next day, Won Pil Kim took his painted picture to Ju Won a bit timidly. Would he like the painting?

A Little Peace

"If he likes it, I will be happy enough," he decided, "even if he does not think it is good enough to pay for." He held it out uncertainly.

Ju Won looked at it, and immediately his face broke into his biggest smile.

"It's great!" he said. "You are really very good. Here, I want to pay you fifteen won instead of ten."

Won Pil Kim was surprised and very happy, indeed.

"Thank you, thank you," he said gratefully.

"Would you like to do more?" asked Ju Won.

"Sure." Then he would be able to offer more money to Sun Myung Moon.

That night, Won Pil Kim took home several photos. As he drew and painted, Sun Myung Moon again sat with him, watching, encouraging, even giving suggestions. It was about midnight when he finished.

The next day Sun Myung Moon had the paints already laid out when Won Pil Kim arrived home. When the work was finished, Won Pil Kim immediately fell into an exhausted asleep. The next morning, everything was cleaned up and put away and the pictures were rolled up neatly, ready to go. Sun Myung Moon had done this for him during the night.

A couple nights later, Won Pil Kim was delayed and got home later than usual. When he came in sight of the hut, he saw Sun Myung Moon standing by the path peering into the darkness.

"Oh, good," said Sun Myung Moon with relief. "I was getting worried. Are you alright?"

"Yes," Won Pil Kim answered, "Everything is fine. It just took a little longer to find pictures to do, that's all." Then Won Pil Kim thought to himself, "He really is like a father to me."

He sat down to work on the pictures. This time Sun Myung Moon surprised him by picking up a brush himself. He started brushing color onto the background of each picture and Won Pil Kim painted the people. They finished a little earlier that night.

As the days went by, Sun Myung Moon also helped paint the clothing. Won Pil Kim drew the pictures and painted the faces, and Sun Myung Moon added little details, such as lines in the hair. In this way, they could finish a picture in twenty minutes, and they were able to do fifteen to twenty pictures in one night. Even so, they sometimes didn't finish the work until well after midnight.

This was their life. After a hard day's work at the army base, Won Pil Kim would come home and they would paint together. Sun Myung Moon had had his own long day of prayer, witnessing, teaching, cooking, shopping, and cleaning, yet he was always by his side while they worked on the pictures through the late hours. They were doing it together. This made Won Pil Kim feel strong.

When the last picture was done, he drifted off to sleep to the sounds of the night. He heard Sun Myung Moon beginning his prayers, and his heart surged with love. Sun Myung Moon's voice fell around his ears like a gentle hand, telling him to rest now for tomorrow's work. Knowing that Sun Myung Moon was praying in the night, caring for him and for others, and knowing that hewas doing his own work well and hard gave his mind rest—and a little peace.

A new kind of work came to True Father and Won Pil Kim to help them sustain themselves as they tried to establish themselves in Pusan.

The Grandmother

Sandra Lowen

"Grandmother Ook," as Mrs. Se Hyun Ook is known, met Sun Myung Moon in Pyongyang and became one of his very first followers. She attended Sun Myung Moon for the rest of her life. Mrs. Ook met Sun Myung Moon on November 11, 1946—before he went to Hung Nam prison, before he went South to Pusan.

She was a very religious woman. She and her husband held important positions in their church. Her eldest son had gone to fight in World War II, and she prayed for him every day. Even after the war, she continued her daily prayers.

One day, she received a revelation that she should meet a certain special man and that she should go to the mountains to pray for more direction. Mrs. Ook was a good Korean housewife. There was washing, cooking, cleaning, mending, shopping—so much to do.

"After I get these things done," she vowed. "Then I will go."

But the jobs never came to an end. Day after day, she put off going to the mountains.

One day she knew she could wait no longer. She just left her work and went. She prayed a long time on a mountain, and the spiritual world soon told her where to meet this certain special man. She followed the directions given her, and she found the little room in

Pyongyang where he stayed. He welcomed her, served her tea, and immediately began teaching her things about the Bible. His message was so powerful that she knew in her heart she wanted to work with him. It was, of course, Sun Myung Moon.

She still had her work at home, however, so the only way she could spend time with Sun Myung Moon was to sneak away. Then, when she was with him, she would forget about time, and the hours flew by. Sometimes days went by! When she returned to her family, they would be very angry. At first, she wouldn't tell them where she had been, but when they later found out about Sun Myung Moon, they told her she shouldn't go back. They thought she should be content with her own church and her household chores. Therefore, she was not able to visit Sun Myung Moon for long periods of time, but she missed him terribly.

Sun Myung Moon missed her, too. He worried about her and longed to talk with her. Once, he resolved to go to her house to see if he could catch even a glimpse of her. He stood outside her house and watched the balcony where she hung out the family wash. He knew that she was a good housewife, and would have to do the laundry soon. Although the day was passing, he was so hopeful of seeing her that he waited and waited. Finally, she came out, not knowing Sun Myung Moon was there. He saw only her back. Still, this it was enough for Sun Myung Moon to know that she was all right, and so he returned home.

A few days later, Mrs. Ook was preparing food for her family. As she reached out to place wood on the fire, she heard a spiritual voice say, "Why are you here? Your Messiah and Lord is suffering. Do you think I called you just to make rice for your family?"

At that moment, her hand began to shake. She couldn't stop. When her family found her shaking, they became frightened. What was the matter with her? They tried to help her, but nothing worked.

The Grandmother

She told them, "I heard God's voice telling me to go to teacher Moon and help him with his work. And then I started shaking."

Her family was very upset. They still didn't like this Mr. Moon, but what could they do? She couldn't just be left there in the middle of the floor, shaking. They held a family meeting.

"She must not be allowed to go to this Mr. Moon!"

"Yes, but if she doesn't, she could die here!"

"Don't be silly! I never heard of anyone dying from shaking!"

"Me either. But this is a spiritual thing. She isn't just sick."

"You're right. Who knows what could happen?"

"I say we send her to Mr. Moon."

Finally the decision was made to let her go. Immediately, Mrs. Ook stopped shaking and ran off to get ready. She was going to be with Sun Myung Moon at last!

Many spiritual people came to Sun Myung Moon after receiving information from the spirit world.

One day, a lady came and said, "I am a very spiritual person and my mother is, too. We were told spiritually to come here. Will someone please tell us all about this group?"

The early disciples told her many things. The next morning, very early, the communist police arrived. That lady was a spy, and she had gone straight to the authorities and told them terrible, untrue things about Sun Myung Moon. When Grandmother Ook came early the next morning, she found Sun Myung Moon, Won Pil Kim, and two ladies being taken away. Mrs. Ook was also placed under arrest and questioned, but her family hired a lawyer and paid for her release.

When Sun Myung Moon was sent to Hung Nam prison, Mrs. Ook traveled the long distance several times to visit him. He was there so long, almost all his disciples in Pyongyang lost faith in him. They thought he would never return. Yet whenever Sun Myung

Moon asked Mrs. Ook, "How is everyone?" she would always answer, "They're fine." She couldn't bear to give him bad news, especially when she saw how he was suffering.

He wore such miserable clothing and had become so thin! She always brought a meal of rice and clothing for him, even though she knew he just gave it away to the other prisoners.

Sometimes he would be moved to another location, and she couldn't easily find him. Just before the Korean War began, she could receive no word of him at all for a while. Sometimes she and Won Pil Kim journeyed to the prison work sites, and he was nowhere to be found. They would ask the prisoners about him and they wouldn't know where he was. Then the spiritual world would tell them that he was still alive.

Later—during the time Sun Myung Moon, Won Pil Kim and Jung Hwa Pak were making their long journey from Pyongyang to Pusan on foot—Grandmother Ook went to Pusan with her family and lost touch with Sun Myung Moon. She had been in Pusan just a few months, working and caring for her family, when one day a young man appeared at her door. It was Won Pil Kim.

"Teacher Moon sent me to find you," he said simply. Those were the most welcome words she had ever heard. Her heart soared. He had been looking for her for quite awhile and had learned where she lived from a Christian minister.

"Tell me," she said excitedly. "What kind of clothes does he have on?"

"He's wearing old green pants, a ragged jacket, and rubber shoes—the same things he always wears. Why?"

Mrs. Ook shook her head. "Those are the same clothes he wore in North Korea. First, I will make him a new set of clothes. Then I will visit him."

And she did.

From that point on, she went to the mountain to be with Sun Myung Moon as often as she could. She helped with his cooking and cleaning so he could have more time for spiritual work. She climbed the hill to the little shack many times. Later, when they set up a tent beside the shack so more people could gather to pray, she was often there. When there were people to take care of, she was there. When there was something urgent to pray for, she was there.

Sun Myung Moon loved her so very much—his dear Ook Halmoni.

True Father's great love for his disciple pulled her close to him in spite of her family's opposition and separation due to the war.

The Missionary

Sandra Lowen

Mrs. Hyun Sil Kang was a religious lady who met Sun Myung Moon in Pusan. She attended a Presbyterian seminary, which was very strict with its students. They were taught to follow the Bible exactly. They did not buy or sell anything on Sundays. They did not drink wine or eat rich foods.

One day, Mrs. Kang heard of a young man who was teaching "strange things" in the mountains of Pusan. She thought to herself, "The Bible speaks of many people who will try to trick others into losing their faith in the last days. Well, these are the last days. Could this be the big deceiver, the Antichrist himself?"

Mrs. Kang couldn't get the idea of this young man out of her mind. She thought Satan must be deceiving him. She also thought of his eternal soul. "He is a child of God, too," she thought. "Someone should try to help him."

Every day, Mrs. Kang prayed three or four hours and read at least 30 pages of the Bible. Every day, she visited at least three homes to talk to the people about God. Perhaps she could save the soul of this young man on the mountain. She did not know how she would find him, but she had faith that God would lead her somehow.

The Missionary

On May 10, 1952, she got the inspiration to go out. As she walked around, she saw a middle-aged woman near a stream. This woman greeted her and asked, "Do you work somewhere?"

Mrs. Kang answered, "I am a missionary."

"I would like to invite you to come home with me."

She wasn't quite sure why she did it, but Mrs. Kang agreed to go. The woman by the stream was none other than Grandmother Ook, and she led Mrs. Kang straight to Sun Myung Moon's little shack on the hill. When Mrs. Kang saw the shabby hut where Sun Myung Moon lived, she could not believe her eyes. It was so terrible; she wondered how anyone could live there without developing a resentful spirit. They went inside and sat down, and soon Sun Myung Moon came in. Mrs. Ook introduced Mrs. Kang to the rather ragged young man, and then she left them together.

Sun Myung Moon took one look at her and said, "God has been giving you so much love for the last seven years."

Mrs. Kang was shocked. It was seven years ago that she had promised her life to God! How could he know that?

Then he said, "Today is a most special day, and you are very fortunate to be here." She could not know it then, but Sun Myung Moon had just finished writing the original Divine Principle.

Sun Myung Moon began teaching her about "The Last Days of the World" and "The Second Advent of the Messiah." He explained that the Messiah would not come on the clouds as she had been taught; he would come as a physical man to their own Korea. As Sun Myung Moon spoke, Mrs. Kang thought to herself, "Well, that would certainly be nice, but the things he says are impossible."

Sun Myung Moon told her that in 1950 Jesus had appeared in the skies of North Korea and during the Korean War, an airline pilot saw Jesus very clearly in the sky. The South Korean newspapers even printed articles about it. Mrs. Kang was disturbed by Sun Myung Moon's words, but she was even more disturbed by his shouting. He spoke with great force, even though the room was very small and she was the only person there. She leaned away from him, and still his booming voice annoyed her. When she looked into his face, she saw that his eyes shone brilliantly, and she wondered if something was wrong with him.

Or maybe something was wrong with her! Oh, dear! Mrs. Kang didn't like having such scary thoughts. She thought, "I've got to get away from here!"

She stood up to go, but Sun Myung Moon asked her to stay for dinner. She said no, but he insisted. Now Mrs. Kang felt even more frightened. Korean standards for conduct between men and women were very strict. She should not even be in the house alone with him, and now they were to have dinner together! But she did not know how to say no and hoped that at least the meal would be good.

It was terrible! No rice at all, just barley—the cheap kind that the government gave out to refugees. There was sour kimchee and bean curd. Sun Myung Moon asked her to pray. How could she pray over such an awful meal? Besides, she was exhausted. So Sun Myung Moon prayed.

That prayer changed Mrs. Kang's life. Never had she heard of such love for God or such dedication to His work. Mrs. Kang realized the difference between her own selfish prayers and his simple offer of his life to God. Mrs. Kang asked if she could come back, and Sun Myung Moon answered, with a smile, that she would be welcome 24 hours a day. In a few days, she returned, and Sun Myung Moon explained more things to her.

One day she was to lead the service at her seminary. She told Sun Myung Moon she had to leave early to prepare for it. However, he

The Missionary

kept talking for so long that she barely made it back in time. She was sure she would do a horrible job of presenting her program because she'd had no time to prepare. Instead, it went splendidly, and everyone told her how inspiring her talk had been. Later, when she told Sun Myung Moon about it, he said that since she'd had no time to pray, he had prayed for her.

Still, it was not easy for Mrs. Kang to be a disciple of Sun Myung Moon. She had so many doubts. But whenever she doubted him, she would feel separation from God. Sometimes she even felt pains in her chest and head. Then she would repent, and the pains would disappear. The day came, however, when Mrs. Kang felt she could not go on. She went to tell Sun Myung Moon she had to leave him. He met her outside the shack.

"You came to tell me you're leaving. But I beg of you, don't leave! I need you so desperately."

Mrs. Kang felt afraid. This man knew everything about her. She didn't even have private thoughts!

He continued, "No one would choose to go such a difficult way, not even I. But it's the way God is calling me. I can't help it. If anyone else were given this mission, I would help that person. Won't you help me?"

Mrs. Kang's heart was softened. But many things still bothered her. For instance, why was Sun Myung Moon so shabby? Why did he live in this ugly hut, disgraceful even for a refugee? Why couldn't he make money?

"Pray about it," he told her, reading her thoughts. "I tell you, someday even Western people will listen to the Divine Principle."

She went home and asked God what to do. The answer came clearly: "This man's situation is just like Jesus 2,000 years ago. Jesus' disciples helped him. Now you should help this man."

She had to obey.

Soon afterwards, Mrs. Kang witnessed to another missionary she had known. This lady had a dream. She saw three balls of light, then three Rose of Sharon flowers (the Korean national flower), and then Jesus' face. Then she saw a mountain, a small refugee hut, and a young man coming to meet her. Mrs. Kang told her that her dream meant that light comes from Korea and that Jesus would appear in Korea. She then took the lady to meet Sun Myung Moon. When the woman saw the hut, she realized that it was the same one she saw in her vision and that Sun Myung Moon was the young man.

Sun Myung Moon told the lady that the vision was not really for her but for Mrs. Kang, to help her stop doubting so much. That lady became a disciple, and she later teased Mrs. Kang.

"I am actually your spiritual mother, not your spiritual daughter, because it was my vision that saved you."

"Maybe so! Maybe so!" Mrs. Kang would laugh. She just knew she was glad she could serve Sun Myung Moon; she was glad she was saved from doubt, and she was glad to be someone who could help the Messiah while he was beginning his work on earth.

True Father's poor physical circumstances bothered Mrs. Kang, but finally she learned to take Heaven's viewpoint and see True Father from Heavenly Parent's eyes.

The First Pioneer

Linna Rapkins

"We're going to make some changes," announced Sun Myung Moon one day in July of 1953.

Won Pil Kim, Mr. Aum, Mrs. Ook, Mrs. Kang and the few others present glanced at each other and then lowered their eyes respectfully. Changes? What could this mean?

The little group in Pusan had now moved into a place somewhat larger than the stone-and-boxes hut built by Sun Myung Moon and Won Pil Kim. People were coming all the time to hear Sun Myung Moon's lectures and to pray with him. It was a busy place, but the people who were dedicated to working full-time with Sun Myung Moon were very few.

"That's right, changes," said Sun Myung Moon, in response to their questioning thoughts. "It's so very important that we quickly reach more people. I know we're not really ready to be separated, but we just can't wait until we're stronger and more able. It appears that the war in Korea is ending. They've called a cease-fire. Nothing definite, but at least there's hope. It should be a little easier to move around now."

He looked at Mrs. Kang and asked, "How would you like to be my first pioneer and work in the city of Taegu? It's about halfway between here and Seoul and is almost as big as Pusan."

"I can do that," she answered.

Sun Myung Moon looked serious. "It won't be easy, of course. You'll be alone, and you have received no real training to be a pioneer. We can't give you much money—just the bus fare to get there and maybe a few won to tide you over. But it is very important to reach more people about God's revelation." He studied her face. "Do you really think you can do it?"

"Yes, Teacher," she answered, without hesitation. "I would be honored to have this mission." She thought of all those years she had witnessed to people in her old church before she met Teacher Moon. It had been excellent training.

"Good," Sun Myung Moon said quietly. Perhaps he was feeling a little sorry, knowing how difficult it would be for his first pioneer, especially since she was a woman and would be working alone. Perhaps he was also thinking how much he would miss her.

He turned to the others. "The rest of us will continue for now in Pusan." Then his eyes focused on Won Pil Kim. "You know, Won Pil, we're together now. We live together, work together, share our meals—but this cannot continue forever. In fact, these days of being together will end sooner than you think."

Won Pil Kim was too startled to speak. This was getting scary. They had been together so long and had been through so much together that any other way of life seemed impossible. They were a team—a unit. They were one. Won Pil Kim thought of Sun Myung Moon standing outside the hut to welcome him each evening when he returned from work. This was his wonderful father figure who took care of him, and this was his teacher who raised him up. How could he live apart from him? He thought about it, but no! He couldn't imagine it.

Again, Sun Myung Moon's heart ached at the thought of separating from his dear disciples, but if they separated and went to several

The First Pioneer

cities, they could meet more people. God's work had to come first.

Mrs. Kang worked alone in Taegu for awhile. She witnessed to many ministers. She witnessed to other people, too, but she couldn't convince anyone to believe her when she told them about Teacher Moon and the Divine Principle.

Finally, Sun Myung Moon decided to help her. He left Pusan. Once he arrived in Taegu, it didn't take long for Sun Myung Moon to make a big impression on the town, and once again he was in trouble. He just prayed and taught God's message day in and day out and through the nights. This was his usual schedule. Then spirit world would send people to him.

Many of those who came were nice ladies who became very inspired by Sun Myung Moon's talks. Whenever they came, they had many spiritual experiences and became so excited, they didn't want to end it and go home. They felt light and happy, and they just wanted to sing and pray and never stop. Many times, they stayed late into the night.

Soon, as you might expect, angry husbands were waiting by their doors when the wives tiptoed home late at night. It was just like the earlier days in Pyongyang, when jealous husbands made so much trouble. Sun Myung Moon felt worried for these ladies, but he couldn't tell them to stay away. God needed them.

Things got worse and worse. Then one of the women came to Sun Myung Moon's place one day, and her face was bruised and swollen.

"What happened?" asked Sun Myung Moon, afraid to hear the answer.

"My husband beat me because I came home so late last night," she answered.

"Oh, I'm so sorry!" Sun Myung Moon said, as tears came to his eyes. "Please be careful." He wanted to tell her to stay home, but he couldn't.

A few days later, another woman came with blood running out of her mouth.

"It's alright, Sun Myung Moon. Don't worry about me," she said, holding a towel to her mouth. "My husband doesn't understand why it is so important for me to come here."

Sun Myung Moon just wept for her. He felt so sorry that these women had to suffer this way.

The next day, another woman arrived, and her hair had been shaved completely off. She was bald! No Korean woman would ever let herself be seen with a bald head.

"My husband thought that if he shaved off my hair, I would be too embarrassed to leave home," she explained, not knowing whether to laugh or cry. "But I would feel dead if I stayed away. Please don't make me go home." And Sun Myung Moon didn't.

The next day, one of the women came with no dress on. She had thrown a blanket over her shoulders and had run like that to Sun Myung Moon's place.

"My husband hid all my clothes so I would have to stay home," she explained. "But I'm here anyway!" There was a triumphant and determined tone in her voice.

Soon word was going around town that women were running naked to Teacher Moon and staying all night with him. It was a huge scandal. Sun Myung Moon couldn't witness to new people anymore or continue teaching because the whole town seemed to believe he was an evil man.

Finally, in September, 1953, Sun Myung Moon told his followers, "Perhaps the rumors will die down if I leave Taegu for awhile. Please work together, all of you. Mrs. Kang will be in charge." He looked at her lovingly. "I will be depending on my hardworking missionary—my first pioneer—to bring results for God in this city."

Sun Myung Moon returned to the heart of Korea—the city of Seoul—while the others stayed in Pusan and Taegu. He had tried to start his work there almost ten years earlier and was thoroughly rejected. Then he had moved north and suffered many things in Pyongyang and Hung Nam prison. A few years later in 1951, on their way south to Pusan he, Jung Hwa Pak, and Won Pil Kim had passed through Seoul. They had seen the city overrun with soldiers and army tanks, with most of the other people heading further South. No one wanted to be around when the communist soldiers arrived.

Now, on a pleasant autumn day in October, 1953, Sun Myung Moon once again entered Seoul. What met his eyes was not so pleasant. Where little houses and busy shops had once stood along the winding roads, there now lay piles of rubble. There were bombed-out shells of old buildings and little footpaths winding in and out among the piles of broken tiles and household items.

The rest of the world had already done much of its rebuilding following World War II, but in Korea there was the Korean War, and it had still been a time for tearing down, not building up.

Sun Myung Moon remembered the Korean myth about the phoenix bird who rose up out of its own ashes to live again. Now Korea must rise up from its own ashes and live again. Looking at the miles and miles of destruction, however, it seemed impossible.

"Oh Seoul! Seoul! Look at you! How many times I tried to reach out to you, and you wouldn't listen!" The pain that stabbed his heart brought tears to his eyes. "How long before laughter and happy voices can fill your air again—your streets again—your homes again. Homes? Can you really call these shacks and lean-tos 'homes'?"

Sun Myung Moon observed ragged families rummaging through the garbage for bits and pieces. The sparkle had left their eyes. The years of war and hunger had worn them down. Sun Myung Moon wandered around with tears flowing down his face. He wanted so much to shout to everyone about the coming new age for Korea and the world. He wanted to give them hope. He wished he could be a big mother hen and gather them all under his protective wings.

If he had stopped to think about it, Sun Myung Moon could very easily have felt hopeless about his own life. He could have said, "I'm already past 30 years old—and look at me. I have nothing—no money, no nice clothes, no job, no family, no home. Other people are poor, but at least they have their families. I have no wife. I have no children. Poor me!" He could have thought this, but his thoughts, as always, were for other people—and for Heavenly Parent.

The days passed by. He kept praying every day, spending long hours alone on mountaintops near Seoul. Spirit world sometimes sent people right up to him, and then he told them about God's message. His heart would reach out to them, and as he taught them, he gave them all the love and power he had. It was very difficult, however, to convince anyone to listen. Most people were just trying to survive.

For two months, Sun Myung Moon worked in Seoul. Besides his busy schedule of praying, witnessing, and teaching, there was another topic continually on his mind—his disciples in Pusan and Taegu. There were no telephones, so he couldn't talk to them.

"How are they doing?" he wondered. "I miss them so much—Mrs. Ook, Mrs. Kang, Mr. Aum, my dear Won Pil. I've never been separated from him since I got out of prison. I wonder how he's doing. I wonder how they're all doing. I wonder if they've found new people. Maybe I shouldn't have left them alone."

In December, he could bear it no longer. He would make the long trip to Pusan and pay a visit in time for Christmas.

In this story we see how True Father was extending his heart in many places and how his disciples were willing to risk theirs to unite with him.

An Island of Purity

Linna Rapkins

It was 1953. The Korean War was ending. Eleven year old Hak Ja Han should be finishing sixth grade and preparing for Middle School. Instead, she found herself standing on a big island called Jeju.

It came as a shock to her when her mother suddenly got this strange idea in her head:

"We are moving away from Taegu," she had announced one day. "The war is ending, so we don't have to stay in the South any longer. Grandmother can live with uncle, and you and I will go to Jeju Do (Island)."

Hak Ja Han's eyes had opened wide in disbelief. "What about Middle School? I'll be entering it in just a few months." She couldn't imagine not being in school.

"Well, our plans have been changed. We will live on the island," was all her mother had said. There was no further discussion.

Now that they were on the island, Hak Ja Han still didn't know what it was all about. She wandered around a bit, looking at the mountain above her. The dead volcano disappeared into the clouds every morning, and she wondered if she, too, was disappearing into the clouds. There were no friends here, no school, no lively, noisy streets; nothing to make her feel normal and alive.

"Why am I here?" she whispered to the wind. "I miss my friends so. Why am I here?" she said to the field of yellow flowers. She turned and saw the dancing sea meeting the wind-swept beach. "Waves going everywhere. Waves going nowhere," she called to the sea. "But at least all you waves have each other."

"Hak Ja-Ya! Hak Ja-Ya! Come here!" It was her mother calling her, just about the only voice besides her own she ever heard any more.

"I'm over here, Omma," she called back politely, but without much enthusiasm. She walked toward her mother.

"Today we will climb higher on the mountain and have a long prayer," was the message her mother brought.

"But, Omma, we just prayed this morning," she answered. Prayer was different now. It had been nice when they went to church at five in the morning and prayed out loud with a whole crowd of people. Then she felt good. But here, on this strange island, it was lonely, lonely, lonely. The wind sounded lonely. The mountain looked lonely. Prayer was lonely. She really wanted to be brave, but suddenly her eyes filled with tears and overflowed onto her sad face. Her Mother felt a pang in her heart when she saw such sadness.

"Am I doing the right thing?" she asked herself, almost ready at that moment to give up and go home. "But no, I must train her to be disciplined. She must learn to give up things that aren't important. She must learn to have her own connection with God so that no matter what is happening, she will be strong. She shouldn't depend on other people to make her happy. And, anyway, I have to keep her away from the boys."

"Come along," she said aloud, ignoring the tears. "God is waiting."

She started up the moutain. Hak Ja Han followed. She had learned obedience well.

"When we get back," said her mother, "I have a new book about the saints for you to read."

Well, at least the books were enjoyable. In fact, they were more interesting than anything else on the island.

As they hiked, they looked for plants to eat. They lived on whatever they could find—no meat, no mandoo (dumplings) or kimchi, and certainly no candy. They were vegetarians now. Thank God it was a tropical island, and they could always find fruit and vegetables.

Even though this was the warmest part of Korea, when the winter winds came, their warm clothes and comforters were not always enough to keep the chill from reaching their bones. Still, the biggest problem of all was the constant loneliness. Her heart felt heavy, almost collapsed. She didn't skip around anymore, or laugh or sing. She did learn to get up early every morning, pray long hours every day, persevere, and obey.

One morning, after prayer time, her mother had a surprise. "We will go back to the mainland today," she said. "All we have to do is pack our things, and just as soon as the next boat comes, we're off."

Hak Ja Han looked at her mother. Was it really true? She waited motionless, wondering if it was a joke.

Her mother started packing. Then she turned and looked at her daughter as if she heard her thoughts. She seemed to ponder something a moment.

Then in softer tones, she said, "I know it has been difficult for you here. But I just happen to know that it is very important for you to live a pure and disciplined life. It's the only thing I knew to do. But this morning I very clearly heard God tell me to take you to your grandmother and uncle." A twinkle came to her eyes. "I guess

He feels sorry for you."

Hak Ja Han's eyes brightened.

"Yes," continued her mother. She was smiling now, but there were also tears in her eyes. "I planned for us to stay here much longer, but God really wants us to go. Grandmother and Uncle are living together in Choon Cheon city now. It's not too far from Seoul and will take us two days to get there. I still think the Lord—you know, the Messiah—will be found in Seoul, but for now we can go to Choon Cheon. Well? What do you think?"

Hak Ja Han broke into a smile, a little skip, and then a hop, and soon she was dancing around for the first time in months.

"Oh yes, oh yes, oh yes," she sang to the sky. "Dear Grandmother, dear Uncle. I will see you soon."

She danced up to her mother. "And I want to see streets and shops and people—and meat. Yes, meat. I'm hungry for lots and lots of meat—and some fresh kimchi to go with it, Omma?"

"Sure, daughter" said her amused mother. "You shall have everything."

"Annyong haseyo, Halmoni! Annyong haseyo, Ajoshi (uncle)." Hak Ja Han said hellow and bowed and then ran into the arms of her grandmother and uncle. Her grandmother's tears fell on her granddaughter's head as she held her tightly.

Soon big servings of bulgoki (Korean style beef slices), white rice and kimchi were ready. It tasted heavenly and after they had eaten every last grain of rice, Hak Ja Han ran to the corner store to buy some sweets.

People were crowding through the streets, getting in each other's way, pushing to get the scarce taxis. Street vendors sat over their burning cinder blocks to keep warm.

An Island of Purity

"Everything is wonderful," she whispered happily to the crowds.

Hak Ja Han had to finish sixth grade that year in order to enter Middle School as planned. Before long, therefore, she settled down into the daily routine of study. She put her mind to work quickly and was obedient and well-disciplined. In her spare time, she liked to draw and sing.

Now that she was away from the island, she could think more fondly of the peaceful beauties to be found there. She drew the delicate flowers she had seen, the billowing clouds drifting in from the sea, the thin morning clouds wrapping around t he mountain peaks. She sang of mountain flowers and dawning days and blue skies.

She was feeling more calm and sure of herself now and more in tune with God's vibrations. Yes, nature had taught her a lot. She would never be alone as long as Heavenly Parent showed Himself in these ways.

Even though she was very lonely on Jeju Island, Hak Ja Han learned to love nature and to turn to Heavenly Parent rather than things or people whenever she felt lonely or in need.

The Crippled Teacher

Chris Garcia

Let's play a game then.
Just you and me.
Let's do it this way:
We'll pretend you're not who you are; you're a different person. You're a Korean person, and you live in Seoul, Korea, and it's a long time ago when your parents were the age you are now—probably the late '50's or early '60's. Got that right?

It's summertime, and it's really hot. You are walking fast because you have to be somewhere special, and you can't wait to get there. There aren't any cars or buses in this area, and you have to walk a long time to get anywhere. You're almost there. You pass a little store on the corner where the old man sells fruit and dried fish out of wooden boxes. You look for him because the streets don't have names or signs, but you know that when you see him, you're almost there.

You wave and say, "Sugo haseyo, Halaboji," which means "You're working hard, grandfather." He's not your grandfather, but that's how you always say hello to him and all older men. You come to the little side street, and you turn into it. Children are playing some kind of game in the dust. Down the little street is the house you've

The Crippled Teacher

been looking for, the place where the crippled man teaches about God.

He's a special man. There's a sign hanging in front that says, "The Holy Spirit Association for the Unification of World Christianity." It's a big name for such a little church. In a way, it's not even a real church. It's a broken-down old house, where the teacher lives. It's where people meet to learn about the teachings called the Divine Principle.

You run to the door, and someone opens it even before you knock, because to them, you are special, and they've been waiting and praying for you a long time. You feel good. They're terribly poor, these people, but you love them dearly, and they love God. They call God "Heavenly Parent."

They're so excited to see that you have come, and they bring you into a room with a chalkboard on the wall, like in school. But this chalkboard is hung close to the floor because the man who teaches here can't stand up very well. Sometimes he leans on his cane to teach, but often he has to sit. Sitting on the floor is also difficult for him, and sometimes he even lies down while teaching. Strange, isn't it?

When he sees you, he tries to get up, but you quickly bow to him and sit down to save him the trouble and pain. The teacher is Mr. Hyo Won Eu. He's a real person, and in real life he was one of the first lecturers of the Divine Principle. What that means is that he was the very first person, besides Sun Myung Moon, to teach the Divine Principle to people. A lecture is a talk about something. A lecturer is someone who teaches.

You sit there waiting for the other people to get settled, and you think, "What if he gives a lecture about Jesus today? The way he tells it always makes me cry because it's such a sad story. But it also makes me realize how much God loves us all." Then you have an idea. Perhaps today I should get up enough nerve to ask him about his own story. "I'd really like to know more about him. Maybe when his regular lecture is done, I should ask him. Maybe he'd be surprised. Probably people don't ask him about his own story. Maybe he'd really like to tell it but is too modest to volunteer."

Mr. Eu's life had been difficult. He had wanted to know about God so much, it almost made him crazy at times. He was a very educated man. He had a logical and scientific mind. That means he could think things through and figure things out. It was hard for him to believe anything unless it made clear sense to him. So he studied and learned and he had many, many thoughts going through his mind. "How do things work in this world? Why were things created this way? Why were they created at all? Did God create them? If there is a God, why can't I see Him?" And so on and so on.

Mr. Eu had an inquiring mind and liked to learn about everything, but the most difficult thing for him to study was the Bible. So many things in the Bible seemed mysterious to a scientific person such as he. It didn't always make sense to him, and it didn't seem to fit with what he knew about science.

Mr. Eu also had a disease in his bones that made him crippled, so he couldn't do much work. In fact, he could hardly even walk. Much of his time, therefore, was spent studying and thinking.

He thought about God a lot and wished he could be a person of God. But how could God ever use a crippled man for much of anything? It was very frustrating to have a mind so bright and a body so weak. Many times, he felt there was no hope for him in this world and many times, he even thought he might just give up on himself.

At those desperate moments, he would always remember something. When he was a little boy, his mother had loved him so very much and had prayed for him every day. She believed in him. Thinking of her, he would then decide not to give up on his life.

The Crippled Teacher

Then one day a friend came to him and said, "I met a very interesting man, Hyo Won. His name is Sun Myung Moon. He's a teacher, and the things he teaches about the Bible are astounding. He seems somehow to know the answers to all the mysteries in the Bible. You should check it out."

Mr. Eu wasn't very interested. No one could understand the mysteries of the Bible. Later, his friend sent two older women to visit him. Perhaps they could convince him to go hear these teachings. As soon as they explained a few things to him, he started asking questions. His questions were so difficult that they didn't know how to answer them. They tried, but they couldn't answer such a scientific mind and educated man. They started crying. They stood over him and just cried and cried and silently prayed for him.

He sat there thinking, "Who are these women, anyway? And why do I feel this strange feeling going through my body? Like heat. Like electricity. My heart is pounding. I feel like crying, but I mustn't. Men don't cry."

Finally, he felt he just had to go with them. But why? He couldn't answer that, but the inner tug got stronger and stronger. His mind wasn't touched, because they hadn't answered any of his questions, but something spoke to his heart.

He went with the old ladies to a small house. He couldn't just get up and go, of course. The house was on a hill, and the hills in Pusan are very steep, so he had to have two men carry him. They brought him into the little house, and he had to lie down on the floor because sitting was too painful.

The group of disciples at that time were few in number. Mrs. Kang was in Taegu and Sun Myung Moon was in Seoul. That left Mr. Aum, who was away at his job a lot; a few older women, like Mrs. Ook; and Won Pil Kim, who was very young. Since Sun Myung Moon was gone, Won Pil Kim was the only one available to teach. To Mr. Eu, he appeared to be just a kid.

Won Pil Kim seemed rather nervous, and when questions were asked, he didn't seem confident to answer them. Mr. Eu didn't know what to think. "Are these teachings worth listening to or not?" he asked himself. "Why am I here? Where are the old women?" But he kept feeling that strange tugging on his heart and that strange sensation of heat and electricity. Mr. Eu's inner struggle showed on his face. Won Pil Kim noticed it and felt badly that he couldn't lecture as well as Teacher Moon. He really wanted Mr. Eu to understand that the Divine Principle was God's most wonderful message in the world.

Then he had an idea.

"Mr. Eu, would you like to borrow these notes on the Divine Principle and study them for yourself?"

Mr. Eu's face brightened. "Could I?"

"Yes, of course. It was written by our honorable teacher, Mr. Moon. It's the only copy we have, but I would really like for you to study it."

Mr. Eu took it home with him. He read it. He read it again. He studied every word. It made sense! It did explain the mysteries of the Bible! It explained the mysteries of life. He still had a lot of questions, but he knew he wanted to join this small group and work full-time for God. He was the very first person to become a disciple without meeting Sun Myung Moon in person.

Mr. Eu eagerly looked forward to meeting this great teacher. When Sun Myung Moon came for a visit from Seoul in December, 1953, Mr. Eu met him for the first time. He was quite surprised to see that Sun Myung Moon was younger than himself, but it wasn't long before he saw that age didn't matter. He asked Sun Myung Moon directly all the questions that were on his mind, and Sun Myung Moon answered them all. After Sun Myung Moon's Christmas visit, Mr. Eu felt he should move to Seoul with Sun Myung

The Crippled Teacher

Moon. This he did right away.

After they found a small house with a room for meetings, Sun Myung Moon spent many hours with Mr. Eu, teaching him, training him, helping him to understand the Divine Principle. Mr. Eu developed diagrams and descriptions that would make it easier for people to understand. Sun Myung Moon was by his side, making sure everything was accurate.

Mr. Eu soon became the official lecturer. Even though his body hurt, he gave lectures all day long, every day. Over and over, he taught Heavenly Parent's Truth. Even if nobody came, he continued lecturing to the spirit world. A person might look in and see him teaching an empty room and wonder what he was doing. Sometimes he stood with a cane; often he sat.

Sometimes, he even had to lie down to teach because of the pain in his body.

In the beginning, Sun Myung Moon listened to all the lectures, and sometimes he helped Mr. Eu explain some point or answer a question. At times, he would cry. Sometimes Mr. Eu would cry and continue lecturing through his tears. It was alright for a man to cry.

Mr. Eu took all his lectures and all the knowledge he had learned from Sun Myung Moon and wrote the Divine Principle book. It was the first time Sun Myung Moon's notes had been made into a book so that people could read it for themselves.

Mr. Eu later became the first President of the Unification Church. Therefore, we call him President Eu. He loved Sun Myung Moon, and he always felt badly that he couldn't bow to him. In fact, he loved him so much, he went out and had a special operation just so he could offer a bow of respect to Sun Myung Moon at least once in his lifetime.

The life of this brilliant, crippled man had been completely changed. No longer did he think of giving up on himself. Even though his body was weak, God could use his bright mind to teach others the Divine Principle. God always has a way of using a person if that person really wants Heavenly Parent to.

In 1970, President Eu went to spirit world. But whenever you hear a lecture on the Divine Principle, or whenever you see the Divine Principle book, you can think of him. And somewhere in spirit world, he's standing on his own two feet—strong and straight—and he's teaching the Divine Principle to all your good ancestors—and probably mine, too.

Mr. Hyo Won Eu's strong mind struggled over his weak body. When he found the Divine Principle, his heart had to struggle over his strong mind. When his heart won, he became the first great teacher, after True Father, of the Divine Principle.

The Unification Church is Born

Linna Rapkins

Sun Myung Moon's surprise Christmas visit to his little group in Pusan turned into a wonderful and inspiring 21-day revival. On the 22nd day, Sun Myung Moon prepared to return to Seoul, so Mr. Eu packed his things to go, too. He had become a disciple before actually meeting Sun Myung Moon, and now that he had spent 21 days with him, Mr. Eu knew he wanted to be Teacher Moon's helper forever and work by his side.

When they arrived in Seoul in early 1954, Mr. Eu quickly found a small place where they could live. Right away, Sun Myung Moon began thoroughly teaching Mr. Eu the Divine Principle. They also prayed long hours that people might be led to their place. Mr. Eu quickly learned how earnest Teacher Moon was about his mission and how hard this work would be.

Before long, a few people did start coming—one here; one there. This was good, but it wasn't enough. Sun Myung Moon knew it would be important to get the Christian churches to help him, so he and Mr. Eu went to Christians again and again, telling them about God's new message and praying deeply for them.

Despite their hard work, however, the same thing happened as before. The Christian people heard Sun Myung Moon teaching about God and Jesus. His stories were different from what was taught in their churches, so they thought Sun Myung Moon must be sent by Satan. They stayed away.

During this time, one of the men who had become a disciple in Taegu arrived in Seoul to join Sun Myung Moon. We know him today as David S.C. Kim, once the President of Sun Myung Moon's school, the Unification Theological Seminary in Barrytown, New York in America. This man had been a high-ranking government official under Syngman Rhee, then South Korea's president, for fourteen years. He wasn't like any government man, however. He was also very spiritual. God had saved his life during the war and had given him a spiritual experience he couldn't forget. He really wanted to work for God, but he wasn't sure how. He went to church faithfully and led the choir, but he knew there had to be more to a spiritual life than that.

When his friend, Mr. Aum, suggested to Mr. Kim in February, 1954 that he should visit Sun Myung Moon's little group in Taegu, he did. After hearing the teaching, and after a couple of inspiring spiritual experiences, he became a disciple. When Sun Myung Moon appeared in Seoul, then, Sun Myung Moon welcomed Mr. Kim warmly and put him right to work.

One day soon thereafter, Sun Myung Moon seemed to have made up his mind about something.

"The people in the churches still do not want to work with me," he told Mr. Eu. "If I have no church, I cannot bring Christians together. If I can't get Christians to work together, the same thing will happen to me that happened to Jesus: I will be killed, and the Christians will go through terrible suffering."

Mr. Eu was very disturbed to hear this, but he didn't know what he could do to help.

"So," continued Teacher Moon, not waiting for an answer, "we will just have to create our own church and start from the beginning."

Mr. Eu's eyebrows went up. This sounded like a good idea, but would it be possible? It was just the two of them in Seoul.

Understanding his thoughts, Teacher Moon added, "It would have been much easier if the churches had united with me, but I just can't wait for them any longer."

Mr. Eu didn't dare think over all the possibilities. He simply gave Teacher Moon the support he needed and nodded his head.

The building they found for their new church didn't look like a church at all. It was old and rickety. The front door was warped from the rain and lacked of paint, so it was difficult to open and close. The roof looked wavy along the top because the building was sinking in some places, and some of the tiles were missing from the roof. Holes in the walls had been patched over with old boards, and many of the paper windows were torn. Strangest of all, half of the building was painted red!

Sun Myung Moon and his little band were not daunted, however. They scrubbed the building from top to bottom. Then they set to work painting a sign that proclaimed who they were: "Holy Spirit Association for the Unification of World Christianity." After nailing it in place, they stood back to admire their handiwork. Suddenly, they burst out laughing. The sign was almost as big as the building itself.

"Is this a good place to unite Christianity?" asked Sun Myung Moon.

"Absolutely," answered Mr. Eu and Mr. Kim jovially.

They bowed their heads then and thanked Heavenly Father for their church, which later became known by a shorter name: the Unification Church. The day Sun Myung Moon's group of disciples became a church was May 1, 1954. After this day, they looked for people to join the church and become members.

Their days were busy, indeed. There was no figure standing over Sun Myung Moon, telling him what to do. Sun Myung Moon didn't wait to be told by Heavenly Parent what to do. He took responsibility to figure out what must be done, and then he did it, knowing Heavenly Parent was supporting him.

Sun Myung Moon followed his regular schedule. Every morning, he rose before the sun and climbed one of Seoul's mountains to pray. For him, prayer was even more important than food.

Mr. Eu worked hard, too. Teacher Moon wanted him to do all the teaching, so he studied the Divine Principle for long hours. He outlined it. He drew diagrams to help explain it. He prayed over it. And soon he was the official teacher. During his lectures, Teacher Moon sat by his side, and Mr. Eu could feel his support. He knew Teacher Moon was praying for him all through the lecture. If a guest asked difficult questions, Teacher Moon would sometimes help Mr. Eu with the answers.

Before long, there were six disciples living with Sun Myung Moon, sharing one room and the three old blankets they owned. They ate from one bowl. In fact, they did almost everything together. But in spite of this encouraging beginning, the time came when they couldn't convince anyone else to come learn. Day after day, no one came to hear about the Divine Principle.

"Hyo Won," said Sun Myung Moon one day. "What do you plan to do today?"

"Pray and study and witness," said Mr. Eu.

"Not teach?"

"There's no one to teach, Teacher Moon. "

"Hyo Won," continued Sun Myung Moon. "I want you to teach anyway. "Mr. Eu tried not to show his surprise.

"From now on, I want you to teach every day, even if no one comes," continued Sun Myung Moon. "This will make a good condition for people to come. And don't forget—spirit world is always listening."

The Unification Church is Born

"Yes, Teacher," promised Mr. Eu. "I will teach."

Day after day, they prayed and witnessed. Day after day, leaning on his cane for support or sitting in a chair, Mr. Eu lectured long hours, pouring his heart out to the thousands of people in spirit world. Still, no people came. It became more and more difficult to do anything. It was like trudging through thick mud, with their feet getting heavier and heavier. Everything was indemnity. It was hard to keep going.

"Is it going to be just the seven of us forever?" They wondered, "Maybe we're crazy after all."

Sun Myung Moon worried about them. Could he keep them from leaving? "Just don't give up," he urged them. "Hold on. Things will get better—I promise. You can do it." He reminded them, "Heavenly Parent loves you very much. He doesn't want you to have to suffer, but you're the only helpers Heavenly Parent has right now, so you're the most important people in the world."

Sun Myung Moon also sang with them a lot. Soon there was one song they sang over and over which became their favorite:

> Jesus walked that lonesome valley;
> He had to walk it by himself.
> Oh, nobody else could walk it for him;
> He had to walk it by himself.
> Jesus had to stand his trial;
> He had to stand it by himself.
> Oh, nobody else could stand it for him;
> He had to stand it by himself.
> We must go and stand our trials;
> We have to stand them by ourselves.
> Oh, nobody else can stand them for us;
> We have to stand them by ourselves.

They sang it over and over and over—twice, three times, twenty times, thirty. Then they felt stronger and more determined.

Sun Myung Moon promised them, "By the end of October we will find more people to join, and they will be very good quality people, too."

Even so, there were many days when they could find nothing more hopeful than his words.

October arrived, and just as Sun Myung Moon had promised, new people began coming. The six months of indemnity were paying off at last, and it was easier to feel hope.

Mr. Eu had to lecture longer hours now—all day and into the night. The more he taught, the more he felt the inspiration that Sun Myung Moon had always felt, and he continued teaching long after exhaustion should have set in. The days went something like this:

Guests arrived for lectures in the morning. They heard lectures until noon. They took a break for lunch. Then back they went into the little lecture room to sit on the floor all afternoon, listening to one long lecture. Dinner came and went. Then Mr. Eu and the others gathered around the guests, bowing and smiling pleasantly.

"Please, won't you stay for the evening? There are some interesting things we would like to explain to you now."

Sun Myung Moon had learned that whenever guests went home after only one day, they always got involved with their family problems and hardly ever returned. He tried to convince the guests to stay at least three days. Some of them did.

Even though the Korean War was over, there was still a curfew of midnight in Seoul. This meant no one was allowed to be outside after that time. Mr. Eu always got so inspired during his lectures, he seemed to forget about time and curfews. Soon it was 11:00, then 11:30. The guests fidgeted nervously, but he just didn't stop. Just when he seemed to be ending the lecture, he announced, "Now, I want to introduce you to our honorable teacher, Sun Myung Moon, the one who received this revelation from God."

The young man, who had been sitting silently beside Mr. Eu or in the back of the room, stood up and bowed to them. All day the guests had seen this young man in the simple clothes, and they thought he was just one of the members of this church. Since Mr. Eu was doing the teaching and seemed to know all the answers, and since he looked somewhat older and was sometimes sitting in a kingly-looking chair, they assumed he was the leader. Once they got over their surprise, however, they were happy to meet this mysterious young man named Moon. As soon as Sun Myung Moon began speaking to them, they could feel his power and his love, and they wondered why they hadn't known before who he was. They felt as if they never wanted to leave.

Sun Myung Moon liked to ask his disciples to sing for the guests. Some of them had voices that were not exactly soothing, but they sang with such love, it was as if Heavenly Parent was singing. The guests felt something beautiful stirring in their hearts. Soon it was well after midnight.

"Oh, I'm so sorry I kept you too long," Sun Myung Moon apologized. "Is it too late to go home?"

They nodded their heads, not knowing what to do, and not really wanting to leave.

"Well, then, won't you please stay here for the night?" he asked. They had no choice but to accept his invitation. If they went home after midnight, they would be arrested for breaking curfew.

They all slept on the floor. Whenever there were only a few people spending the night, there were enough quilts to go around. But when many people stayed, the quilts couldn't reach over all of them, and they had to depend on their body heat to keep them warm. The next morning, basins of cold water were brought for washing their faces.

Then, after a simple breakfast, someone would say, "Please stay for another lecture—okay?"

"Well, I've stayed one day and night already," they reasoned to themselves. "I guess another lecture won't make much difference. But I wonder why I don't even want to leave." It felt as if a loving blanket had been tucked around them.

After another day of lectures, the same routine happened: listen to Sun Myung Moon speak, eat some rice and kimchi, sing some songs, share some thoughts, curfew, too late to go home. Alright, sleep under the quilts. The third day—same thing. Mr. Eu lectured all day. By evening, the last lecture came to an end. When the guests stood up to go, the family members brought out special cakes and cookies. Well, they couldn't refuse those now, could they?

The feeling in the air was like heaven. They gazed around the room as they ate the little cakes, wondering why they felt as if they might float away. Love filled the air; it filled their hearts. They couldn't explain it. They just knew they felt something very good.

At home that night, they were soon brought down to earth by the familiar problems of work and family life. Still, even after several days, they couldn't forget Sun Myung Moon. They began plotting how they could return.

Sun Myung Moon pushed himself to do more and more. Just when he thought he couldn't move another inch, he moved another mile. He always felt desperate to find more new members and to keep the members he already had. Sun Myung Moon prayed for the members day and night. He spent many hours with them, teaching them all he knew. He forgot about himself. Whenever someone brought food to him, he might eat it absent-mindedly or he might not get around to it. Many days, he forgot to eat anything at all—one day, two days, three days; he didn't really plan to fast; he just forgot to eat.

Sometimes he took everyone up on a mountain to pray. They prayed in unison for a long time, their voices growing louder and louder, their bodies shaking and swaying in the cold wind. Sometimes their words joined together into one voice. It seemed as if they were all saying the same thing, all together, in the same rhythm. They felt as if they might float up into the air, and they forgot the coldness of the wind. While praying, some of them opened their eyes a moment, and they noticed Sun Myung Moon gazing off into space with a sort of faraway look, his eyes shining as if he were seeing a vision. They looked up into the sky, too, but they saw only clouds. One woman was spiritually open, however, and she saw Jesus come down on a cloud and talk to Sun Myung Moon. Bright lights were everywhere—around Jesus, around Sun Myung Moon, around the people. It was dazzling.

Sun Myung Moon became very tired. After weeks of keeping this kind of schedule, he reached a state of exhaustion. His eyes became red and scratchy from lack of sleep, and at times, he couldn't even open his eyes fully in the sunlight. He felt like closing them and sleeping for at least a year. His bones ached, his muscles ached. He even had a problem with his nose bleeding, he was so worn out. His throat hurt from talking so much, and he got canker sores in his mouth and on his tongue. When he talked, it felt like fire. Some of the people noticed this and wept for him.

"Please, get some rest," they begged. "You don't have to talk to us tonight."

They wished they could somehow make it easier for him. Sun Myung Moon appreciated their love, but he still felt the weight of the world on his shoulders, and he could not rest.

This was the humble and difficult beginning of Unification Church in Seoul, Korea. Yet greater difficulties were just around the corner.

This story tells of the labor and difficulties True Father and the newborn Unification Church and its members were having in the very earliest of days. Through their sacrifices, this tiny church began to grow and eventually spread around the globe.

An Encounter with Ehwa University

Linna Rapkins

In Seoul, there were several universities where young students studied for their careers. One of these universities was for women only. Its name was Ehwa University, which means, in English "Pear Blossom" University.

Mr. Eu was witnessing to everyone he knew, and one of these people was his relative, Mrs. Yang. She was a music teacher at Ehwa University.

When he first told her about Sun Myung Moon and the new revelation, she didn't want to go. After all, university professors are very important people. They have to think of their reputations. Still, she was curious about the changes in Mr. Eu's life, and one day, her curiosity got the best of her. Mrs. Yang was a rather spiritual woman. She could sense what was going on around her spiritually, and she could often feel whether something was good or bad, whether it was from God or not.

She listened to Mr. Eu's lectures politely, but skeptically. As the minutes and hours passed, however, she felt a strange excitement growing inside her.

"I feel God in this place," she was thinking. "And the teaching makes a lot of sense."

When the last lecture came to an end, suddenly without warning, she jumped up before the little group and sang a song. She had never heard this song before, and neither had anyone else! Spirit world was singing through her. It was as if the room came to life. Everyone caught the feeling of joy and felt like dancing and laughing and singing and they did! It was a great moment.

Mrs. Yang's life was changed that day. When she returned to the university, she told many people about her experience. Even though she was a respected professor, she didn't care anymore what people thought of her. The word soon got around at the university that a young fellow in a dilapidated house was teaching something interesting, and people were getting inspired. Students started investigating. They told others about it and the numbers multiplied.

Those who came felt something spiritual happening in their lives, and it became hard for them to concentrate on their studies. They returned again and again when they should have been studying their lessons. Soon the teachers began to notice a change in their students.

"Why are so many of the girls absent lately?" they asked each other. "Is there a sickness going around?"

"I don't know of any sickness," said one. "Anyway, they never stay home just because they're sick."

"True, true," responded another. "Besides, their minds seem to be off somewhere else all the time."

"Yes, and their eyes sparkle," complained still another.

"One of them told me she is visiting a man who teaches new things about the Bible—and something about the Messiah coming to Korea—now."

"Sounds like some wild-eyed fanatic!"

"It certainly does," they all agreed. They decided to report it to the officials in charge of the university.

The president and the administrators talked it over then. How much should they be worried? After a big discussion, they decided they would take a wait-and-see attitude. Perhaps the students would get tired of going there, especially since many of them were in their final year and were looking forward to graduating.

Then some parents got word that their daughters were spending time with a very strange man. The parents got very worried. It was a great privilege to attend a university. The parents had worked hard during all those years of war and had made many sacrifices in order to send their children there, so they didn't want anything to go wrong now. They were very upset and went straight to the university president to complain.

"We didn't send our girls here to run off with some crazy man," they stormed. "We want you to put a stop to it—now!"

"Yes, yes, of course," agreed the president. "We'll take care of it right away." He certainly didn't want the university to get a bad reputation.

The very next day, an announcement was made: "Students may no longer go to Sun Myung Moon's church. It is off-limits starting today."

Some of the students obediently stopped going. But by now, many of them were on fire for God. All their lives, they had been taught to obey their parents and teachers, but for the first time, they understood that God should be obeyed first. So they continued going to Sun Myung Moon's little church, sneaking out of the dormitory every chance they got. Soon they were outcasts at the university. No one wanted to sit near them. No one wanted to be seen talking to them. Everyone seemed to be afraid of them. You would think they had leprosy or something.

Meanwhile, the administrators decided to try another tactic. They would send one of their teachers to hear the lectures; then this teacher could explain logically to the students what was wrong with the teachings. Intelligent students would listen to reason.

When the chosen teacher arrived at the little church, she listened very carefully and took many notes. By the end of three days, however, she got so inspired that she became a member herself! The officials at the university were in a rage. How could this happen? What was going on, anyway?

They decided to send another professor. Again, there were the lectures, the notetaking, and the three days. Then the same thing happened—the professor joined the church!

The frustrated administrators still didn't want to give up. What to do? What to do? They decided to send one of the most important people at the university—their respected Dean of Students.

Again, God worked. This lady's heart was moved, and she became one of the most devoted and most beloved members ever. Her name was Mrs. Won Bok Choi.

The administrators just couldn't believe this was happening! They talked it over at length and decided to try just one more time. They chose a professor who had studied Christianity and other religions. She had graduated from three seminaries and was very intelligent. She was also the type of person who was logical and who didn't get emotional about things. She was expected to become president of Ehwa some day. This woman would never get swept off her feet by some crazy preacher. She was Miss Young Oon Kim.

She was quite ill from a kidney disease, but she agreed to check it out. She found the little church and, taking off her shoes, she entered without a word. Her face was serious as she sat down for the lectures. Sun Myung Moon sat beside Mr. Eu, his eyes lowered in silent prayer.

An Encounter with Ehwa University

In the next room, many of the members, especially the students and teachers from Ehwa, gathered to pray for her. They drilled a little hole in the wall so they could take turns watching her. This would be a crucial set of lectures, because, if she went to the president with a negative report, that would be it for them. They would be forbidden to attend the church forever. They prayed really hard all through Mr. Eu's lectures. She listened politely, but what was she thinking? No one could tell. On and on went the lectures—one hour, two hours, three, four. Nothing happened. She just listened and took notes.

Then Mr. Eu came to the part about spirit world. As he described the spirit mind and spirit body, life after death and so on, she looked a little more interested. No one knew that she had been trying for years to find out more about spirit world. She had been greatly inspired by a man named Emanuel Swedenborg, who had written a book about the spirit world. It was a great book, yet it did not answer all the questions she had. In fact, she had found no one who could answer them. Now, Mr. Eu was answering all her questions. On the outside, her face looked interested, but calm. Inside, she was feeling growing excitement.

After the lecture, she hid her excitement and asked many questions. She even debated with Mr. Eu, trying to prove him wrong, but he had a good answer for every question. When Sun Myung Moon spoke to her, she felt even more inspired.

As the three days went by, she noticed that while she was at the church, the pain from her kidney disease disappeared. When she went home in the evening, however, the pain returned. In the days ahead, whenever she doubted the Divine Principle and argued with Mr. Eu and Sun Myung Moon, the pain got stronger, but whenever she believed, the pain went away. Finally, she had to admit this was God's answer to her lifelong prayers. She decided to join this little church of few people who said they would change the world.

Meanwhile, the university president was anxiously awaiting her return. When she finally arrived with her report, it wasn't what he wanted to hear at all.

"I have studied the Bible for many years and prayed for answers," she began. "Now I know it was all for the purpose of finding this man, Sun Myung Moon. It was all preparation to help him. It has been made clear to me that he has been sent by God to do even greater things than Jesus."

When he heard these words, he was greatly disappointed, to say the least! You just didn't say things like that in a Christian school.

"Good-bye, Kim Sonsaeng-nim" (professor), he was barely able to utter. "With you or without you, I will end this craziness."

That very day, he summoned the students and professors who had joined Sun Myung Moon's church to a meeting.

"Students and teachers at Ehwa are expected to conduct themselves in a respectable manner at all times," he said. "And you are a disgrace to our university—the scum of the earth. I should just kick you out here and now, but, out of the kindness of my heart, I have decided to give you one more chance. I'm giving you a choice. Choice number one: if you stop going to Moon's so-called church today, you may continue to attend the university. Choice number two: if you do not stop going, you will be expelled from school, effective immediately."

This was a most difficult choice. Attending a university in Korea meant earning lots of money and having a comfortable life. It was right after the war, and they knew what poverty was like. Some of these young ladies had studied very, very hard for many years just so they could attend university. Their parents had made big sacrifices for them. They talked it over with each other, and many decided they couldn't give up graduation, after all. Out of 100 or so students, there were fourteen brave women who decided to stand by Heavenly Parent and Teacher Moon.

"We love Heavenly Parent now. We love Teacher Moon, and we believe the Divine Principle is true," they affirmed. "No university president can force us to give it up." They were expelled from the university. In the case of the five professors, they were fired. Their positions had paid well and brought them much respect, but now it was unlikely that they would ever have another chance to teach in a university. As they walked out, their heads were held high, and they smiled. They felt as if they were being decorated by heaven. A gold star from heaven is a million times more valuable than a diploma or job at Ehwa University.

When they arrived back at the church, they were received as heroines. That night there was a great prayer meeting, and God touched each one of those brave women. As they prayed, they were given the gift of prophesying about the future, just like the early Christians after the death of Jesus.

They could never fully explain to anyone else exactly how they felt; it was such a deep feeling. But whenever they looked into each other's eyes, they understood each other. And whenever Heavenly Parent and Teacher Moon looked at them, they understood—and loved them dearly.

Sacrificing their education and future prospects of wealth and great careers, fourteen brave young women from Ehwa University chose to go with Heavenly Parent and True Father. For this, they got diplomas from Heaven and many spiritual gifts.

Jailed

Linna Rapkins

It was May, 1955 when the fourteen young women were evicted from Ehwa University. Around this time, Won Pil Kim and Grandmother Ook arrived from Pusan to join the Unification Church in Seoul. It was a most interesting time to arrive, because by this time, Seoul was in an uproar over Sun Myung Moon. It had started with the events at Ehwa University and was followed by worse and worse persecution. Now, all Seoul seemed to be out to get Sun Myung Moon and his Unificationists.

The newspapers had heard about the students being kicked out, and they wanted interviews. They had heard rumors that once a person went into Sun Myung Moon's church, they never came out again. Day after day, they hovered around the church building, badgering the members with questions and trying to snap pictures of Sun Myung Moon.

"Who is this dangerous fanatic?" they asked again and again.

"Why would you give up your education for a crazy man? Did he lock you up? Did he torture you?"

"Does he hide your shoes so you can't leave?"

"Does he keep all the young pretty girls in a back room?"

"He's an electrical engineer, right? Did he install an electrical gadget that brainwashes people?"

To make their stories more interesting, they often added details of their own invention. One story proclaimed, "There are three doors at Unification Church. When you go through the first door, you have to take off your shoes and jacket. When you go through the second door, you have to take off your outer clothes. When you pass through the third door, you have to take off everything!" Then the headlines screamed, "Naked people stay in basement of Unification Church!" It didn't matter to them that no one had ever seen a naked person there or that the building didn't even have a basement!

There was one woman who kept wondering about all the rumors. Were they true? What if they were just lies? What if God did speak through this man? She really wanted to know. But what if the rumors were true? What if she went there and they took off all her clothes? That would be just too terrible. Still, she couldn't get it off her mind. One day she gathered up all her courage and prepared to go to the church to find out what it was all about. Over her long Korean dress she put on a second set of clothes, and over that she put on a third set of clothes. That way, if they started taking her clothes off, maybe she could escape with some of them still on.

Filled with fear, she entered the first door. The members welcomed her warmly. She took off her shoes voluntarily, because that's what you do in Korea. No one mentioned taking off anything else. She went trembling through the second door. Nothing happened. And then the third door. She still had all three sets of clothes on! Then she sat down for the lectures and learned the truth about the Unification Church. Soon she was a member.

There were people who remembered Sun Myung Moon from Pyongyang or Taegu, and they spread some of the same old lies about him. Negative parents of the students wanted him arrested, and they filed a court case. Things were really getting hysterical.

On July 4, 1955, the reporters were especially annoying.

"This must be the Day of Persecution," observed Mr. Eu. In the evening, when two investigators showed up at the rickety door, he knew he was right.

"Where is Moon?" they asked. "We want to ask him some questions at the police station."

Sun Myung Moon came to the door. "You can ask questions here," he offered. "Please come in."

The investigators paused a moment, looking around a bit fearfully. "Well, we have our car right here. We can just take you to the station where there is more privacy. We'll bring you right back," they promised.

Sun Myung Moon consented and Mr. Eu and Young Oon Kim went along. They were both thinking the same thing: "He might need us."

At the station, however, they were not allowed to go into the same room with Sun Myung Moon. Soon one of the investigators nudged them toward the door.

"You don't need to stay," he told them. "We're taking good care of him. We'll bring him back in our car. "

Mr. Eu and Miss Kim went back to the church and waited with the others. But Sun Myung Moon didn't come back. That night, Mr. Eu could hardly sleep. "Why, oh why did I leave him?" he lamented, tossing and turning on his mat, tears trickling onto his rice pillow. "I'm no better than Peter. I failed my Lord. "

The next morning, everyone eagerly awaited Sun Myung Moon's return. They peered down the path, but there was no sign of him. Then someone brought the daily newspapers, and they were shocked to see the headlines: " Sun Myung Moon arrested!"

"That does it," said Mr. Eu, slapping his hand on his knee. "I'm going back. If they arrest me—well, fine, let it be so." He limped out the door. There would be no lectures today.

When he reached the police station, some of the family members were already there.

"Where is Teacher Moon?" asked Mr. Eu anxiously. No one knew.

They waited. They went around buying all the newspapers they could find so no one else could read the lies about Teacher Moon. Then they waited in a nearby teahouse, discussing what to do. When they returned to the station, Mr. Eu was told to go into one of the investigation rooms. As he walked down the hall, he glanced into another room and was shocked to see young Won Pil Kim sitting in a hard chair. An investigator was questioning him and giving him a slap every now and then.

"Why aren't you in the army?" yelled the investigator in his face. "Fellows your age should be soldiers. Did you run away?" Whack! Won Pil Kim struggled not to fall over, but he said nothing.

Soon Mr. Eu was sitting in a hard chair in another room, and they were yelling questions in his face. "Why do you imprison people in your house? Why do you force them to stay three days in your stinky place?"

Mr. Eu answered all the unfair questions the best he could. The room was hot, and his stomach was empty. He felt nauseous, but he could only think how much worse it must be for Teacher Moon. Finally, he was released, and he went back to the church with the other members.

Everyone looked worried and forlorn—like sheep who had lost their shepherd. This persecution was making some of them stronger in their faith and more determined, but some of them were being filled with doubts. Maybe the newspapers were right. Maybe Sun Myung Moon really was evil.

The next morning, the members went to the station to be as close to their beloved Teacher as they could. Praying together and singing the song about "Can even death stop me?" had given them greater courage. Again, they waited as each member was questioned. By the end of the day, Won Pil Kim was arrested. There was still no news of Sun Myung Moon. Four more days went by like this. Then came Sunday evening, and an investigator appeared at the door to arrest Mr. Eu.

"Good!" he thought to himself. "Perhaps now I will see Teacher Moon." Later, however, a disappointed Mr. Eu was released, and he had caught no glimpse of Teacher Moon.

The next day, he and two others were arrested again and held at the East Gate jail. It was the first time in his life he had ever been locked behind bars, and it felt very strange to him. But all he could think of was, "Where is Teacher Moon?"

At dawn, they were taken off to the Chong No City Station—and there, at last, Mr. Eu found Teacher Moon! He greeted him and Won Pil Kim, feeling more joyful than he had felt in weeks as the gates clanged shut behind him.

Before long, the police came in, bound them all together by the wrists, and led them into a waiting car. They were going to court.

As the vehicle pulled out, they saw faithful members along the way. They looked extremely upset and tears were streaming down their faces, so Mr. Eu stuck his head out and told them, "Dear brothers and sisters, don't worry. We're alright. Just pray a lot."

As they struggled out of the car at the station, their wrists hurting from being bound so tightly, Sun Myung Moon didn't complain or look upset.

He said, "We are bound together for eternity. Nothing can ever separate us now. Let us be determined to fight even unto death."

These words gave them strength, and they affirmed in unison, "Yes!" Their voices sounded strong, but Sun Myung Moon turned to Mr. Eu and said, "Hyo Won, you are having a hard time, aren't you?"

Jailed

Mr. Eu bowed his head. He was trying to be cheerful, but it wasn't so easy.

"I'm sorry, Teacher," he said softly. "I just feel that it is because of our mistakes that you are in trouble. You're innocent, and yet you're going to jail." Tears welled up in his eyes, and he tried to wipe them on his shoulder.

Sun Myung Moon just pressed his lips together and seemed to go into deep thought. He loved Mr. Eu and all the others, but he couldn't always show it.

That night they were taken to still another prison—West Gate Prison. They arrived after midnight, tired and hungry, and were herded into Building 6, Ward 9. They were separated into different cells this time, so they couldn't talk to each other. Before arriving, Sun Myung Moon—being experienced in prison life—had told them to memorize each other's cell numbers. Instead of being called by name, they would be called by cell number. This way, they would know what was happening to each other.

It was not pleasant in these cells, but the worst was yet to come. After two days, they were taken to court to be questioned. The police led 24 prisoners, including Sun Myung Moon and the five members, into a little holding room that was barely large enough for two twin beds. It was July 15, the hottest time of the year. They couldn't sit down, so they stood all day, at times leaning against each other for support. Sweat poured down and drenched their clothes. They were hungry and so thirsty their mouths felt like sandpaper. Was this Seoul, Korea or was this hell?

All day they waited, but their numbers were not called, and finally they were taken back to jail. They were kept there for two more weeks. During this time, they felt very close to each other, even though they were in different cells. They each had a tiny high window. Every morning, Won Pil Kim climbed up on the lid of the ceramic bucket which served as a toilet, and greeted Sun Myung Moon with a bow. Sun Myung Moon would see him and bow back. When he did this, Won Pil Kim received more energy for the day.

He decided to do in this prison what Sun Myung Moon had done in Hung Nam prison—to keep a very strict schedule and wash himself every morning with a wet towel. It wasn't as easy as he might have thought. First, he had to wake himself up very early with no alarm clock. Then the guards kept wanting to know what he was doing. So he came to understand something about Sun Myung Moon's experience at Hung Nam Prison, where conditions were much worse.

July 29 came, their 22nd day of prison life, and they were finally brought to trial. Again, they were all bound together and led into the courtroom to be questioned. Those innocent young men, who only wanted to work for Heavenly Parent, whose only desire was to make the world heavenly, were found guilty—guilty of brainwashing, guilty of being with women, and finally, when they couldn't think of anything else, guilty of evading the army. The sentence was announced by the judge.

" Sun Myung Moon gets two years! Hyo Won Eu gets two years! The others get one year!"

Everyone gasped. It was totally unfair.

While they were serving their time in prison, the rumors on the outside kept getting crazier. Many of the members became confused and left. Parents kidnapped their grown children from the church. Newspapers printed wild stories. It seemed like everyone in Seoul hated Sun Myung Moon. After two months of this, there was good news. A member brought the news to the prisoners:

"You will be released this evening!"

"Are you sure?" asked Mr. Eu in disbelief. "Is it official?"

"Yes, it's all set," came the reply.

Jailed

Won Pil Kim was looking out his window. "This evening?" he cried out.

"Yes, this evening," answered Mr. Eu with a loud voice. It sounded so definite, but underneath, no one could really be certain.

They gathered their things. They waited. The evening ticked away. Nothing happened. Finally, disappointed, they lay down to sleep. Maybe tomorrow. Maybe never. You just never knew. Then, in the middle of their dreams, they suddenly heard clank, clank! A door was being unlocked and opened.

A voice shouted into the darkness, "380, come out with all your things!" That was Mr. Eu.

As he passed by Sun Myung Moon, he murmured, "Why me? What's going on?"

"Go quickly," answered Sun Myung Moon. "That's just the way it is, and don't worry about it!"

Tears came to Mr. Eu's eyes as he limped away. Could he leave his dear Teacher? Should he? Before he could think further, church members reached out and helped him into a waiting jeep, and he was on his way home.

One week later, all six men were called to appear in court. This time, a new judge pronounced Sun Myung Moon and Mr. Eu innocent. The others had to finish their one year sentences for evading the army but were pronounced innocent of the other charges. (Actually, Sun Myung Moon appealed this, and the others were released one month later.)

After three months in prison, Sun Myung Moon was free at last! The family members had lined up outside the prison gates to welcome him, and everyone was smiling. They all went back to the church in a rented bus. It was October 4, 1955—a victorious and glorious day!

Another happy event took place three days later: they moved. While Sun Myung Moon was in prison, the family members had somehow scraped together some money and, for the first time, they had their own building. It was an old Buddhist temple on a winding little street in the Chung Pa Dong area. Neglected for several years, it had become shabby and absolutely filthy.

Now that they had scoured it thoroughly, it seemed like a palace. There was a big meeting room where they could all easily assemble. Behind the meeting room were a number of smaller rooms on two levels which could be used for living space. In the front of the building was a stone courtyard overlooking the rooftops of Seoul.

A big celebration was prepared as a "Welcome Home" party for Sun Myung Moon. The treats were passed out by Sun Myung Moon himself—one apple and a few pastries for each person. It was a banquet. Poetry was recited. Songs were sung. And Sun Myung Moon sang songs of heaven.

The heavenly pioneers of this small group were truly bound together for eternity.

Although they faced great persecution, even being put in jail for their faith, True Father and his disciples got through it together, united, and could celebrate triumphant with heavenly joy.

The Princess

Linna Rapkins

Hak Ja Han's mother, Soon Ae Hong, came home later than usual, and there was a new light in her eyes.

"Well, I had a most interesting day," she announced joyfully.

"Where were you, Omma?" asked her daughter, looking up from her studies. Grandmother stopped stirring the soup to listen.

"I met Kim Halmoni's uncle. Do you remember the Holy Lord Order? No, of course not; you weren't even born when I went to that church." They laughed together. "Well, anyway, I met him, and he invited me to a new church. I thought I was dropping in for a little visit, but I was there for hours. The church is called the Holy Spirit Association for the Unification of World Christianity."

"What a long name," observed her daughter.

"Yes—well, they want to bring together all Christians. And guess what? You know I've been talking about the Lord of the Second Advent all your life—right?"

"Right, Omma."

"Well, they say he is here in Korea, just as Kim Halmoni and Mrs. Ho said he would be. They said if I study their book, I will learn exactly who he is." Her daughter listened raptly.

In the days to follow, Soon Ae became very busy. She still had to work to earn money, but she spent every spare moment either attending the little church in Choon Cheon or reading the book, which explained the revelations of the founder and leader.

Whenever she studied the book at home, she would look up often and say excitedly to the others, "He must be a very intelligent man, a very spiritual man. Many of the things I learned at Kim Halmoni's and Mrs. Ho's church, he also says, but he explains much, much more. I can scarcely believe my good luck and great joy."

When she approached her daughter and asked, "Would you like to come to the service with me tonight?" Hak Ja Han was ready.

"I would like that," she said. She wanted to see what gave her mother so much joy.

When Soon Ae officially joined the Unification Church, her daughter joined with her. Except for reading about the saints, she hadn't studied other religions so much, but this felt very right. And as she studied the book, she knew she would dedicate her life to this.

Soon, Soon Ae announced that she wanted to go to Seoul to meet this great man for herself.

"It will take only a few days," she said. "He may be the one I've been looking for all these years, but I can hardly believe it. I just have to meet him."

The grandmother, uncle, and daughter looked forward to her return, for they too wondered what he was like. But they waited a long time, because once Soon Ae got there, she didn't want to leave. She became the cook for the man they called their teacher—Sun Myung Moon. This was 1957.

Meanwhile, although she loved her grandmother dearly, Hak Ja Han missed her mother. A thirteen year old really needs her mother's care. Once again, she felt lonely, but this time she knew how to handle it better. She focused on her studies more than ever and led a very quiet life—almost like a nun in a convent.

When Soon Ae finally came home, however, it was not to stay. She explained everything she had been doing and all about the people in the church in Seoul, and most of all, about Sun Myung Moon.

"He's the one—the one I've been looking for and preparing for. Kim Halmoni and Mrs. Ho and all their followers were looking for this man, but I'm the only one who actually found him." Her eyes saddened as she remembered the sacrifices they had made, even unto death. Well, she would attend him remembering them, and she would teach her daughter to attend and remember, too.

She turned then to her daughter. "Hak Ja-Ya, would you like to go to Seoul and meet him, too?"

"Oh yes, I would, Omma," answered her daughter immediately. "I've been thinking about you and about him every day since you left."

As they made their way to the Chung Pa Dong church, everything in Seoul looked different than Hak Ja Han remembered. There were more buildings; more things to buy; more vehicles of all types; more noise. It was all so interesting.

As they walked up the steps to the church, she suddenly felt as if she were coming home. She felt calm and peace in her heart. Her mother led her into the main room.

"He is upstairs," someone told her, so she led her daughter up some little steps in the back. They tapped on the sliding door and were invited into a room with a man who looked very kind and thoughtful.

Without being told, Hak Ja Han bowed deeply. Then she just stood still, waiting for him to begin the conversation.

"So this is he," she thought as gazed at him. Then she realized he was looking into her eyes.

"You have a very lovely daughter, don't you?" he said to her mother. Then, with a smile, he asked, "Does she study well?"

"Oh yes, she studies very well," answered her mother proudly.

"What is your name?" he asked her directly.

"My name is Hak Ja Han."

There was a pause as he continued to look at her thoughtfully. He closed his eyes a few moments, and then softly, almost as if in prayer, he said, "Oh Heavenly Parent, you have given such a woman, Hak Ja Han, to this country of Korea!"

She looked down at the floor, wondering, "Why would a great spiritual leader say something like that about me?"

Later, after she was back in Choon Cheon with her grandmother and uncle, she thought every day about that meeting. She resolved to be a strong member of this church and to unite him always. She decided she would live her life even more strictly than before, always praying to be pure and good.

As she attended Middle School and then High School, her days were filled with study, art, music, prayer, church—and thoughts about the man in Seoul who was the promised one for Korea, and indeed, for all the world.

True Mother had inherited much from her own mother's dedication and her own efforts to be good. When she met True Father, he knew immediately that she was a very special person.

The First 40-Day Condition

Linna Rapkins

The meeting room in the Chung Pa Dong Church was packed with Unification Church members seated on the wide boards of the wooden floor. The doors had been left open in the stifling July heat in an attempt to catch any breeze that might pass by. But mostly, the soft lanterns attracted the summer bugs and made it very difficult to concentrate.

Teacher Moon was speaking to the members. He poured out all that was in his heart, as he always did. Tonight, he was telling them over and over how special they were.

"You are the ones," he said, "who can save the world and bring joy to Heavenly Parent. Never, never forget that!"

It was not easy to be chosen ones these days. It seemed impossible to bring a single person to a single meeting anymore. The terrible lies and rumors constantly passed around Seoul made people afraid to come.

"You are the ones Heavenly Parent loves most," he continued. "Can you believe it?"

They wanted to believe it, but most of them at that moment felt so discouraged, it was hard to be hopeful. A few weeks ago, Sun Myung Moon had asked them all to do a seven-day fast. Well, now the fast was finished. Perhaps he would let them rest a few days. Perhaps that was the purpose of this special meeting.

"You have completed your seven-day fast," he said. "You made a great indemnity condition through this fast. But, most of all, you learned that you do not live by food alone. You must never forget that your real power comes from God."

He wiped the sweat from his brow. He spoke in a quieter tone, with great love, but almost as if he felt pain. He said, "Now, we will begin something new. You know the meaning of the number 40—yes? We will do a special condition for 40 days."

A 40-day condition? What did this mean? They concentrated on his words carefully, for they had never done a 40-day condition before.

"We will take our message out of Seoul to the other people of Korea. For 40 days, I want all of you to go out to the countryside—to farm villages, fishing villages, everywhere. You will teach the Divine Principle to these people. You will tell them about the importance of Korea. But first, you must serve them. Help them with their work. Suffer with them."

Go out? Suffer with them? How would they support themselves? What would happen to their families? There were many silent questions.

"Yes," he continued, ignoring their questioning eyes. "You are God's chosen people, and this is what you must do."

As they prayed in unison, they were already going over in their minds just how they would do it. Even though the Korean War had ended seven years earlier, it still was not easy to make a living. To leave their jobs and families for 40 days would be very, very difficult. But then, life was always difficult, wasn't it?

Their voices got stronger as they prayed. Their spirits got stronger, and their courage mounted. They were ready to unite with their Teacher.

The First 40-Day Condition

All day, the rented bus jolted and jostled through the countryside. As they pulled into each village, someone was dropped off and everyone shouted, "Annyong!-i kaseyo! Annyong-i kye-seyol (Go in peace! Stay in peace!)" They waved to each other until they were out of sight in a cloud of dust.

Some of the members being dropped off were just high school boys and girls—mere teenagers! Others were college graduates. Still others were mothers and fathers who had left their children with their own parents.

At one village, they let off a high school boy with a crippled leg. He hobbled out of the bus, and as the bus pulled away, he suddenly became afraid and tears came to his eyes. Their hearts cried for him as they pulled away. How would he manage?

It was late afternoon when the bus pulled into an isolated farming village to let off the last passenger. A teenage girl stepped out. Her belongings were tied into a sack that she could carry on her back or on her head. She had a few won and her Bible and Divine Principle notes.

It was a lonely feeling as she said good-bye to the bus driver and team-leader, and she watched the bus until it disappeared around a bend. Only then did she take a look around her.

A few women were busy about their homes, preparing food, gathering charcoal, and bringing in the clean clothes. The grandmothers were mending clothing, chopping cabbage, and watching children. Surrounding the village were the rice fields. Men and women were barefoot in water up to their ankles, bending over the neat rows of rice plants. The flies and bugs tormented them constantly, and the stink of the fertilizer was strong. Sharp pains were no doubt shooting through their backs from bending over all day, but they continued working to nurture the precious plants that provided their main source of food.

Suddenly a great wave of loneliness and fear swept through the girl. She felt sick. "What am I doing?" she asked herself, putting her hand to her stomach. "These people have lived here for generations. I'm just a lost girl to them—a crazy person."

She had always been rather shy, and talking to strangers was never easy for her, even in a friendly situation. Here, they would probably not be so welcoming. No one came up to her. It was as if they sensed something strange. A tear pushed its way down her cheek, and she quickly lowered her eyes so no one would notice. She walked over to a bank leading down to a little creek, hoping to regain her composure. She washed her hands in the water just to have something to do.

She closed her eyes. "Heavenly Parent," she whispered. "I didn't know it would be this hard. Please be with me now. I cannot do this alone." Soon she began to feel a little stronger.

"I pray for these people," she continued. "You have been waiting for 6000 years to help them, and they have been waiting all their lives to meet You."

She climbed up the embankment and headed back into the village. Walking up to the first house, she saw a young mother dumping out some old water.

"Annyong haseyo," she called out, bowing slightly and smiling. The woman paused in her doorway and barely returned the greeting. She seemed uneasy.

The girl walked up to her and said, "I've just come into town for a few weeks. Do you know of any place where I might stay?"

"I don't know of any place," answered the woman.

Undaunted, the girl continued, "I wonder if there is any way I might be of some help to you?"

The mother quickly shook her head and retreated into the darkness of the doorway.

The First 40-Day Condition

The girl went on to the next house before she could lose courage. She called out, "Yoboseyo! Yoboseyo! (Hello! Hello!)" After several minutes, an old man hobbled out. She bowed respectfully.

"What do you want?" he asked in a shaky, worn-out voice.

"Halaboji (grandfather), do you have any work that needs to be done?" she asked with the best smile she could produce. "I will be in this village for a few weeks, and I would like to be of some help. You don't have to pay me."

He looked at her suspiciously and waved her away. Disappointed, she walked on. By the time she reached the last house, most people had come home for the night. They seemed to have already heard about her. She couldn't even get the words out before they shook their heads disapprovingly and told her they didn't want any help.

The sun was getting close to the horizon. What should she do? She trudged back to the creek. There was no food for her that night. She sat looking into the slowly moving waters and prayed. She prayed for each person she had met. She asked God what she should do. When the sun had disappeared for the night, she spread out her shawl behind a clump of little trees and lay her head on her bundle of belongings. Soon she was fast asleep, unmindful of the night animals around her.

The next morning, she woke up before any of the villagers. In the early morning grayness, she found an old broom behind a shed. She quickly swept the courtyard where several houses faced each other. She tidied it up and then went back to her spot beside the stream. When the people came out, they noticed the clean courtyard right away.

"What happened?" they asked each other. "Who did this?" It didn't take them long to figure out that it must have been the young stranger. Nevertheless, they continued to ignore her.

The second day was more difficult than the first because, by this time, she was very hungry. At one home, the front room had been made into a sort of store. She went in and bought a big rice ball. She had so little money; she would have to spend it carefully.

She had been brought up in the city in a rather well-to-do home, so farm life was totally new to her. She watched the people throughout the day and saw how hard they worked and how little they had. What a difficult life!

"How can I help these people, Heavenly Parent?" she asked. She concentrated on loving them. Hot tears began flowing down her face. All day she prayed, and every time she thought of the hard life of these families, her tears refused to stop. She came to understand that these were Heavenly Parent's tears. God had seen their suffering for many years, and now God could weep for these people through her eyes, God's tears running down her face.

The next morning, after another night in the clump of trees, she swept the earth around more of the cottages and piled things up neatly. Again, when the villagers awoke, they were astonished. On the third day, she did more cleaning and gathered straw for repairing the roofs. Then she walked around the village and tried once again to talk to the people. She played with the children. One mother talked to her a few moments, and that is how she learned that all the villagers already knew she was from the Unification Church. How they got that information, she didn't know. She went back to the clump of trees and prayed even more fervently for them. By this time, she knew all their faces and could picture them in her mind when she prayed.

In the afternoon, she again walked through the village, and the young mother in the first house took pity on her and invited her in for a cup of tea. A few rice cakes were served. They talked about the children and family life. They talked about the problems of farming. They talked about loneliness and constant fatigue. The mother began to feel she had a friend who understood her—someone who cared.

The First 40-Day Condition

Again, the girl asked, "Isn't there some way I can help you? I really do want to work."

"Well," answered the young mother, unable to resist such a tempting offer any longer. "If you really want to help, I do have a few things." She looked closely at this strange girl. "But I just don't understand why you are doing it. I can't pay you."

"It's alright," the girl reassured her. "I want to do it." Soon she was sweeping and scrubbing floors, washing dishes, and caring for the children. She was happy.

The next day, she went around asking the farmers how she could help. One man handed her a tool and said, "Well, if you insist, maybe you could help with some digging."

She worked hard from morning till night. The people she worked for shared food with her. That evening, the villagers gathered in clumps.

"Why is she doing this?" they asked each other.

"I just don't understand such a person," they said.

"Well, I surely do wish my girl would work that hard," sighed one.

"Maybe she's going to ask for money."

"We'd better not trust her."

Someone approached her and asked, "Who is your father?" If she was from a special family, they would treat her better, but they learned he was just an ordinary person.

They asked, "Did you finish high school?"

"Yes," she answered. "In fact, I graduated from the University."

"You are a university graduate?" they asked, astounded. "But why are you doing farm work?"

She just smiled and picked up a scythe and walked off to cut some weeds before the sun went down. Now their curiosity was getting really intense. The next day they stopped her again.

"Come on. Tell us what you're really doing."

She smiled and answered, "What do you want to know?"

"Everything," they answered. "Our relatives and friends want to know, too."

"Will you gather them all together, and will you let me speak as long as I wish and explain whatever I wish and will you listen?" she asked. She might as well ask for everything while she was at it.

"Alright," they agreed. "We will let you do that."

The next evening, after the usual long day of work, many of the villagers gathered in the largest home. After they were settled, she stood up to speak. It was unusual for a woman—especially a young one and especially a stranger—to speak to a group of men and women. She took a deep breath and began her story.

"I graduated from Ehwa University," she said. "Almost right away, I met a member of the Unification Church, and I learned about a new revelation from God and about a man named Sun Myung Moon..."

They listened. During parts of her story, tears came to her eyes. As she told them about God's heart of pain, she cried. The villagers were touched. Their hearts came to life. First, some of the women began to cry. Then even some of the men let the tears come. They felt the love of God in their hearts.

When she stopped speaking and sat down, the father stood up.

"Even here in our little village, we have heard terrible stories about your church. We thought it was full of evil people. Honestly speaking, we were afraid of you. But I can see now that you aren't evil at all. I feel something in my heart I have never felt before. Do you think you could explain this—what do you call it—Divine Principle—to us?"

The girl could only cry and nod her head happily. "It's what I have prayed for," she said.

The First 40-Day Condition

In the days that followed, she taught almost everyone in the village.

A couple of weeks later, as the girl was working in the rice fields, she noticed a vehicle coming down the road. A vehicle on that road was a rare sight. All the villagers stopped to stare as it pulled into town and came to a stop. It was an American Jeep!

The doors opened on each side and out stepped several men and two women. The man in the lead quickly singled her out and walked straight toward her! His white shirt hung loosely over his pants, and his white hat kept his face in the shadows.

Just then she recognized him and bowed. It was Teacher Moon! She couldn't believe her eyes. With him was one of the church members with a camera—probably the only member who even had a camera—and Young Oon Kim and Mrs. Won Bok Choi. They had bought a Jeep just so they could travel around and visit all the members.

What a day this was! Teacher Moon asked how she was doing and offered to help. She explained that they were trying to quickly get the new crop of rice seedlings planted because time was running out for a good crop.

"I will help," he said, and she almost fainted with surprise. With great swiftness, he rolled up his pants legs, and soon he was wading up to his knees in muddy water along with the villagers. That day she saw Teacher Moon work harder than anyone else under the glaring sun. The planting was completed earlier than expected, and that evening the villagers had a wonderful meeting with Teacher Moon. Only later would they realize what an important event it had been.

When the 40 days were over, the old buses rattled around the countryside picking everyone up. The crippled boy, they learned, had preached in the streets every day and had tried to sell things to get money for food. The people had cruelly ridiculed him, and many nights he had cried himself to sleep. Now, however, safely seated in the bus, he was all smiles. Through his suffering, he had come very close to Heavenly Parent's heart.

When the bus came to the girl's village, her new-found friends had taken time off from their work to see her off. They gave her presents and bowed again and again and cried together. They thanked her for changing their lives, and she felt she was leaving her best friends in the whole wide world.

Back at the Chung Pa Dong Church, Teacher Moon eagerly awaited the return of his beloved people. They didn't know it, but he had suffered more than they. He had spent long, long hours in prayer for them each of the 40 days, agonizing over them and crying for them. It would have been easier for him if he had gone out himself. Several nights, he had even slept out in a field just so he could feel united with their suffering and feel close to them.

A delicious meal was prepared, and when he saw their bright faces, great was his joy. They ate and talked and sang. As they exchanged their stories, they all looked like shining stars from heaven. Their spirits were big and bright. The prayer service that night was very strong, and the spirit of God came down upon each of them. It felt like they got a big, big hug from their Parent in Heaven.

The first 40-day condition was very hard, but with hearts of love and service, the members went out and connected to Heavenly Parent's heart and returned home feeling victorious.

Part 4

Our True Parents

The Bridegroom

Linna Rapkins

The three years between 1957 and 1960 were busy, indeed! Let the papers print their lies. Let the parents complain. Let the people sneer and mock. There was a great feeling among the Unificationists in those early years after their 40 days in the countryside. They had learned that when they worked hard and were persecuted, they received energizing strength from Heavenly Parent.

There were more 40-day conditions, and the stories that the hardworking members had to tell would fill a book. Always, Sun Myung Moon traveled around in his jeep to visit the members and to give them encouragement. More than once, he worked in the villages and made friends with the farmers and fishermen. In many towns, the Unification Church gained new members.

At the Chung Pa Dong Church, things were buzzing with activity, day and night. There were lectures and prayer meetings and meals and discussion groups. The young women often gathered to pray for the men who were out preaching. A choir was begun. A library was created with donated books. Clubs for students and clubs for women were established, and everyone was very busy.

Sun Myung Moon often talked with the members, sometimes taking them to mountain tops where he taught them more about the Divine Principle. During the three years before 1960, he talked to them often about the meaning of marriage.

"The time is coming," he said. "I will be blessed by God in holy marriage, and this will be the most important event in all the world. Then you will be blessed in marriage, too."

This was always an interesting subject.

"It will be a heavenly marriage," he explained. "And there will be a heavenly banquet. The bride and groom will be the new Adam and Eve. They will be the True Parents of all humankind. Then God's side can grow strong, and Satan's side will grow weaker and weaker."

They listened carefully. His bride would be their True Mother. They thought about it. Then the question naturally formed in their minds: "Who will she be?"

They looked around. Well, Teacher Moon was almost 40, so she would probably be a woman in her thirties. That way, she would be younger than he, but not too young. This woman would be the mother of all of them, so she would surely be someone who was respected by everyone.

Perhaps she would be one of the young women from Ehwa University. Yes, that made sense. Those ladies were well educated, intelligent, and came from respected families. They were dedicated to God, and some were beautiful, as well. They were able to be leaders. Yes, this made sense to them.

As they entered the year of 1960, some older ladies who received messages from God came to Teacher Moon.

"We have received messages that your bride has arrived," they said to him.

"Who is it?" he asked.

"We didn't receive the name," they answered. "But it is clear she has arrived." Sun Myung Moon listened but said nothing. He was waiting for a clear sign from God.

The Bridegroom

In January, he announced to the members, "I have received God's message that my engagement must take place by March 1, 1960. We will prepare everything now. Heavenly Parent will show me before then who my bride will be." He would not choose one himself.

The time drew nearer. The clothing and decorations were almost ready. But where was the bride?

After awhile, one old woman went to Sun Myung Moon privately. "I believe I should choose the bride for you," she said.

He paused a moment. He never wanted to answer too hastily and risk missing God's voice. Was God speaking through her? But he felt clear.

"No," he answered, "I cannot allow you to choose someone for me. Only God can do that."

One day, Sun Myung Moon went into one of the rooms of the church where the older ladies often gathered. There were about 40 of them. He paced back and forth silently. No one said anything.

"Has anyone received any messages from God about my bride?" he asked finally.

Oh, how each lady wished she could answer with a "Yes."

Just then, a voice spoke softly and a bit timidly. "A thousand pardons. I have received something."

Everyone turned to look. Why, it was Soon Ae, the cook! She was not one of the leading prayer ladies. And, besides, she was too old to be his wife!

Soon Ae had been receiving a series of revelations but she had told no one. The latest one was a dream, but it was so vivid, it seemed real. In this dream, a bird came down from heaven. Another bird flew up from the earth. In the sky they flew together and became one. Then she noticed that the eyes of the bird from heaven looked just like Teacher Moon's eyes. And when she looked at the bird from earth, she was amazed to see that its face looked like her daughter, Hak Ja Han! When she woke up, she had felt so joyful that, without thinking of her dignity, she just jumped up and danced around the room.

"At last! At last! The world shall have True Parents," she sang. "We are their children! We are their children!"

From that moment, she felt that her daughter was really in the position of her true mother. Every day after that, she not only bowed toward Teacher Moon's room, but she bowed also in the direction of her daughter back in Choon Cheon.

"Yes?" Sun Myung Moon's voice brought her back to the present. "What did you receive, Soon Ae?"

Soon Ae looked a bit embarrassed. Maybe she was wrong for speaking up. But she stood up and bowed.

"I have received several revelations about my daughter," she said.

The other women looked at each other, puzzled. They didn't remember any daughter. A few of them remembered a schoolgirl visiting a few years earlier. That's all.

"Who is your daughter?" asked Sun Myung Moon, looking at her intently, seeming to peer into her very soul.

"Her name is Hak Ja Han," she replied. "She is living with my brother in Choon Cheon."

Sun Myung Moon paused only a moment before replying, "I would like to talk to her."

That very day, a note was written and sent to Hak Ja Han: "You shall hereby prepare for a heavenly engagement and forthcoming wedding." It was the first of February.

The next Sunday, the seventeen year old Hak Ja Han arrived at Chung Pa Dong Church. She had just turned eighteen by the Korean way of counting birthdays. Her mother walked in with her, and they sat down on the floor to wait for the service to begin.

Throughout the service, Soon Ae stole glances at her daughter.

"How grown-up she looks today," she thought. "She doesn't look like a girl anymore. She looks so womanly."

Everything in the church seemed brighter that day. Soon Ae noticed other members looking at her daughter. Most of them did not remember Hak Ja Han's visit four years earlier. Then Soon Ae saw something else. Teacher Moon was looking at her daughter, too. In fact, his eyes were on her throughout most of his speech that day. Soon Ae's eyes moved from Teacher Moon to her daughter. Was the girl embarrassed? It was obvious she knew Teacher Moon was watching her, but her face was serene. She looked as if she had been expecting this moment all her life and as if there were some kind of silent communication going on between them.

When the service was over, Sun Myung Moon walked over to the two of them and gazed at Hak Ja Han for a long while. Then he turned to Soon Ae.

"Please bring your daughter upstairs. I would like to speak with her."

They followed him up the narrow stairs and into his little room. They had barely seated themselves on the floor when he began asking her questions.

"What does your name mean?"

"White crane," she answered.

"Where were you born?"

"Pyung-an province."

He was born in that very same province!

"When were you born?"

"January 6, 1943."

He was born on January 6th, also! There is a saying in Korea that if a husband and wife have the same birthday, they are already special people and their marriage is blessed by Heaven.

"What religion were your parents?"

"Both were Christian."

So were his.

"Do you read very much?"

"I read about the lives of the saints when I'm not studying for school."

"Who is your family? How did you hear about the Divine Principle? Have you studied it? Do you pray? What do you pray about? What is the most important part of the Principle to you?" The questions kept coming.

Soon Ae watched her daughter. She was so young and had not participated in Unification Church life very much.

"Oh dear," she thought. "Maybe I should have stayed at home and prepared her better."

She was soon reassured, however. Hak Ja Han continued to answer the questions very well. Although the meeting went on for about nine hours, she didn't look uncomfortable at all.

Late that evening, Sun Myung Moon ended the meeting. "Now I will get you a tutor," he said. "And then we will meet again."

It was soon arranged for Hak Ja Han to live with Mrs. Won Bok Choi in a little house near the church. Ever since she had left Ehwa University, Mrs. Choi had been a very close disciple. He relied on her for many things. Her heart was deep, and she was just a lovely, lovely person.

Her job as tutor was to prepare this teenage girl to become the True Mother of all the universe. Every day, they spent long hours going over the Divine Principle. Mrs. Choi explained to her the importance of the heavenly bride, the importance of the True Mother, and what she must be like and what she must do. To her amazement, Hak Ja Han understood these things easily. Mrs. Choi discovered that she had been praying and studying every day and had already learned many of the answers. She had kept herself pure. Even her thoughts were pure. She had focused on her studies at school and on spiritual things. She loved God. She didn't talk very much, but she had a sense about what was right and then did it.

During this time of tutoring, Hak Ja Han and Mrs. Choi attended meetings at the church.

One night, Sun Myung Moon unexpectedly turned to her and said, "Hak Ja Han, please sing for us."

Mrs. Choi felt tense. In the back of the room, Soon Ae felt tense. Hak Ja Han stood up. Her red and yellow Korean chogori (Korean style dress) seemed to be the centerpiece of the room and her face the centerpiece of love. She sang a folk song—a love song, really:

"When spring comes mountains and fields, valleys and river banks are decorated with azaleas.

"My mind, too, is blooming like the azaleas.

"When you come and pluck the flowers,

"Don't leave me alone;

"Pluck mine, too."

"Is she too bold for singing such a song to Teacher Moon?" wondered Mrs. Choi uneasily. But Hak Ja Han seemed confident, and she appeared to enjoy singing. Teacher Moon appeared to enjoy listening.

After the service, Sun Myung Moon asked them to come up to his room. He asked Hak Ja Han more questions about the Divine Principle and about herself. Then, handing her a pad of paper, he asked her to draw a picture. She skillfully drew a picture of hills and trees and mountains, with one person in it. Again, Sun Myung Moon looked pleased.

"Tomorrow morning, please come here again," he said.

The next day, Sun Myung Moon took her on a long walk. They went to the mountains together and talked all day. He asked more questions. He explained things to her about the Divine Principle and about his own life. She was a very good student.

When the engagement was announced for March 1 (by the lunar calendar), it was like a big earthquake had hit. Almost everyone was shocked. Of course, they had seen Teacher Moon talking to this teenager, and they had thought she must be someone special—but wife?

"Impossible!" they gasped. "He's 40 and she's only 18!"

"She's too young to be our Mother. How can we bow down to her? How can she lead us?"

"She hasn't even gone out witnessing or anything!"

"And her mother has been in the church only four years! They are just spiritual babies!"

Some of the women had hoped they might be chosen, so it was hard now to be cheerful. Some were just plain jealous.

It seemed that March 1 came in a twinkling, but—miracle of miracles—they were prepared. The decorations were beautiful, and everything was clean and bright.

Just a small group of Sun Myung Moon's closest disciples attended this important ceremony. Sun Myung Moon and Hak Ja Han were dressed in beautiful new Korean clothes. Sun Myung Moon said a long, tearful prayer as he thanked Heavenly Parent for preparing such a woman. After his prayer, he explained to everyone the meaning of the ceremony.

Turning then to Hak Ja Han, he said, "Please say a few words to everyone."

Everyone leaned forward. What would this quiet girl say on such an important occasion? Perhaps she would be so frightened she would not know what to say or even break down in tears.

She stood up and looked at them briefly. Lowering her eyes, she said simply, "I don't have the kind of foundation you have. I know that. But I am being asked to take this role, and I promise you that all my life I will do my very best. I pledge to do whatever I am asked."

She paused and glanced around the room at these older, more experienced members. "But I need your help. Without your support, I cannot fulfill this mission." She bowed to them and bowed to Sun Myung Moon, and she sat down quietly.

The members were touched by her words. Some of the women began to cry. They saw that she really understood her role—to be True Mother to all people. They saw that she was willing to take responsibility for the position of all women. And, even though she was younger than any of them, she was willing to dedicate her life for them.

There was special food for everyone then, and joyfully they shared it. Entertainment followed the meal as Sun Myung Moon asked each one to sing.

At one point, as one member was singing, Sun Myung Moon suddenly got up and started dancing. Happily and with a free spirit, he swayed to the music. Immediately, without any prompting, Hak Ja Han got up and began swaying to the music, too. She looked so natural, and she followed him perfectly, as if she had been dancing with him all her life.

Again, everyone was amazed. Many of them had been with Sun Myung Moon for five years or more, but they knew they could never have been so confident and natural. It was clear that Heavenly Parent had taught her directly.

The heavens were singing a new song that night.

Even though it did not make sense from an earthly point of view, the young and inexperienced Hak Ja Han was indeed the bride chosen for True Father by Heaven.

The Marriage of the Lamb

Linna Rapkins

"The Blessing will take place on March 16," announced Teacher Moon to all the members of the Chung Pa Dong Unification Church.

The women exchanged quick glances full of inner meaning. They already knew there would be a wedding sometime, but Teacher Moon and Hak Ja Han had just become engaged on March 1st, and they had not expected it to happen so soon. That meant there was hardly any time left to prepare all the wedding garments, the food, do the cleaning and decorating, and everything else!

"And furthermore," he continued, "There will be both a traditional Korean ceremony and a Western-style ceremony."

This was surprising news, for they had never heard of such a thing in Korea. Immediately, the women began translating this news into tasks to be done.

"This means two sets of clothing will have to be hand-sewn in two weeks," they were thinking. "Where is the best place to buy the fabric? Who should do the buying, and who should do the sewing?" The wheels were whirring in their heads.

As soon as Teacher Moon left the room, meetings were held to decide what had to be prepared and who would be assigned to each task. Soon they were hurrying in groups to the East Gate Market and South Gate Market for fabric, to the local shi jang (supermarket) for food, and so on. Although they didn't have much money or time, they knew it should be beautifully done. And, most of all, it must be prepared very lovingly and prayerfully.

Even though some of the young women still had not overcome their disappointment in not being chosen as Teacher Moon's bride, they worked from morning to night—and often even through the night—to help prepare for his wedding. After all, this was the "Marriage of the Lamb" mentioned in the last book of the Bible, Revelations. This was the most important moment in the world—the time when God's people would become stronger—and they understood that it was a great privilege to be helping.

As the day drew closer, many of the members became very tired from working through the nights. Their eyes were red from sewing for hours without rest. Then, as if that wasn't enough, they learned that everyone who was invited to attend the marriage ceremony had to wear a new white gown. These gowns had to be made as well.

Soon enough, the sun rose on the great day. The church was cleaned and polished once again, and some of the portable walls had been removed to make more space. It was hard to get flowers, but there were plants decorating the room. On the front wall was a beautifully painted scene representing the world and the whole cosmos. The flags of the world hung from the ceiling. Never had this simple old building looked so beautiful.

The older members, robed in white, silently took their places on the floor, and soon the room was filled with the dazzling white gowns topped by black heads bowed in prayer.

Mr. Eu was the leader of the day—a sort of master of ceremonies. He announced to the people that the ceremony would now begin.

It was still morning when Sun Myung Moon and Hak Ja Han entered the room. Everyone gazed silently at the pair and were once again filled with wonder to see their beloved 40 year old teacher with this young girl who would be his wife. Although by now everyone had had time to become accustomed to the idea, the question still occurred to many of them, "Isn't 18 years just too young for such a position? To be the real mother of the whole world, the whole cosmos, is too huge a mission for anyone, much less a simple, immature girl."

And yet, they had to admit she was radiantly beautiful. She walked gracefully and calmly, her eyes cast humbly toward the floor. At the same time, there was a certain air of self-assurance about her.

This was the Western ceremony, so she wore the beautiful white gown sewn by the ladies of the church. Although it was designed like a Korean dress, the fact that it was white and topped with a lace veil made it Western. In her arms were a few white flowers tied with bows of lace. Mrs. Won Bok Choi followed her and watched out for her gown and the train of lace.

Sun Myung Moon wore an impeccable white tuxedo and a white bow tie. The members had never seen him looking so handsome.

The bride and groom walked together to the front of the room. They took seven steps, which signified going through the Old Testament Age, and stopped with both feet together and bowed. Then they took seven more slow steps signifying the New Testament Age. Again, they stopped and bowed. Their minds were totally focused on the deep meaning of walking through history. Then the final seven steps were taken, signifying the Completed Testament Age. This brought them to the front of the room, and they bowed one last time.

Mr. Eu and Mrs. Choi stood on either side as the couple said their vows before Heaven. There was no minister standing before them to tell them what to say. Everything was directed from Heaven, and Sun Myung Moon said the words and told his bride what to say. Then he prayed. It was a long prayer with tears, for it was a serious occasion.

After the prayer, they walked out of the room together.

Mr. Eu explained to everyone, "We will now wait for the Korean ceremony to be made ready. Let us keep a very prayerful attitude as we prepare the atmosphere for the second marriage ceremony." They all prayed and sang songs as they waited.

When they returned, Sun Myung Moon and Hak Ja Han looked most regal in the colorful Korean costumes with tall headdresses. Their brightness made a striking contrast against the white of the cloth-covered floor and the white-robed members. Again there were the vows and the prayers, with Mr. Eu and Mrs. Choi attending.

When this part of the ceremony was completed, Sun Myung Moon turned to the members and announced that they were now officially blessed in marriage before Heaven. The cosmos and Heavenly Parent finally had True Parents on the earth.

"Now we have been purified before God," he said. "It is the beginning of a new lineage. Therefore, from this moment on, it will be very important to purify everything we use. In fact, once anyone is blessed in marriage, they should use only new things. Actually, we really should grow all our own food, make all our own clothes, even spin our own thread and weave our own cloth."

The members listened carefully. This was going to be a lot of work, so they wanted to understand exactly what to do. Some members, such as Mrs. Hong, remembered Ho Ho Bin's group and how they prepared clothing and food for Jesus and for the Lord of the Second Advent. Would they be doing this sort of thing again? If so, it would be a full time job for several people.

"However," he continued. "This is not practical for us. We have so much work to do to find new members and restore the world to God's original plans for Creation. We cannot spend all our time raising cotton, spinning thread, planting rice, and so on. Therefore, we will continue to buy clothes and food at the market as before. But we will always sanctify everything before using it. For this, I will now create a new purifying salt. We will start a new tradition of putting this special salt on all our new things once we are blessed in marriage. Then, whatever we use will be purified, just as if we made it ourselves. This shall be called 'Holy Salt.'"

He turned to the altar and measured some salt into a special container and said a prayer over it. This was the very first Holy Salt created and all our Holy Salt used today is multiplired from that first supply created at True Parents' wedding.

Then he turned back to the audience and began to speak. Hak Ja Han Moon, now True Mother, sat on the side and listened. Sun Myung Moon, True Father, spoke about the meaning of their wedding. He explained why his bride had to be so young and inexperienced. He explained his new bride would stand in the position of all the roles of womankind—as daughter, sister, wife and finally mother—and that Heavenly Parent is showing True Father how he must be like a father to his new bride and walk her through restoring those roles for all women throughout all time. He explained many things to the members for several hours. It seemed like a long speech to them because they had already been sitting on the floor for so many hours, but he wanted to be sure they understood everything that was happening.

Late in the afternoon, mealtime was announced. It was time for the Banquet of the Lord.

Low tables were quickly set up and the food was carried from the kitchen around to the front door. (There was no door connecting the kitchen into the rest of the building. That way, the smells and sounds of cooking could not disturb the activities in the main part of the building.)

Everything was beautifully prepared. Actually, it was rather simple fare by our standards today. There was some chicken and freshly made kimchee and a lot of rice. Who would have expected that kimchee would be served at the cosmic Banquet of the Lord? But for these chosen people, it was a wonderful treat, for they often had to exist on barley and chopped cabbage sprinkled with red pepper and garlic. Bowls of spring fruit rounded out the meal.

Then True Father said to them, "I wish all of you could take home some mementos of this occasion. However, there may not be enough things to pass around. Therefore, let's draw numbers to see who will get the mementos."

One person's prize was a collection of bones from the chickens. "These bones you should keep forever," directed True Father. "Although you may share some of them with others, if you wish."

To the others, he said, "You should keep the seeds from the fruit you eat here. These are very precious and should never be thrown out."

Then came entertainment. Everyone had a chance to get up and sing. There was singing and dancing aplenty that night. The bride and groom sang and danced together. There was laughter and applause, for although this was a very serious occasion, it was also a very joyous one. The heavens were truly ringing with song and dance and tremendous joy.

The Marriage Blessing of True Parents in holy matrimony was the beginning of a purified world. True Father introduced Holy Salt to emphasize what a new realm members were to live in from that day forth.

Mother's Course

Linna Rapkins

She loved peace and quiet. She loved reading and music. She was intelligent and studied well. Her life was quiet and protected. She was like a lovely, lonely flower living in a greenhouse, away from the rest of the world. Suddenly, she was thrust into the center of a noisy battlefield where those around her were witnessing and trying to restore the world. She was a little raft in a mighty torrent. Hak Ja Han had accepted the role of True Mother for all humankind for all time.

The women of the Unification Church were busy all day the year Hak Ja Han was blessed in marriage to Sun Myung Moon. They cooked, cleaned, sewed, shopped, and in addition to this full schedule, they also found time to go out and tell people about God, the Divine Principle, and about True Father. Some of these hard-working women found it hard to accept True Father's new wife, Hak Ja Han. They knew she was to be the mother of all people. The True Mother. Their True Mother! Yet, the women in the church were all older than she. They had been born earlier and had joined the church earlier.

Some of these women thought, "She's so young and inexperienced. How can we respect her?" A few even felt they could have been a better wife than she. "She was much younger than most of us. I don't think I can call her True Mother," they said jealously. "I bet mother Soon Ae is gloating now that her daughter is married to True Father," said others. They truly loved True Father, and they didn't really want to complain, but jealous feelings were strong day and night.

One day Soon Ae hurried out of the kitchen and around to the front of the building at the Chung Pa Dong church, she finished drying her hands by waving them in the air.

"I wonder why I have been called by True Father," she thought to herself. Now that her daughter was his wife, everything had changed so much.

"I don't know what to do anymore," she murmured to herself. "How should the mother of the Messiah's bride act, anyway?" So far, True Father had not asked her to do anything. She hardly ever saw her dear daughter anymore.

She reached the top of the stairs and turned to the sliding doors of True Father's little room. He waved her in. She bowed respectfully and sat on the mat-covered floor before him.

"Your daughter is well," said True Father, knowing how much she wanted to hear those words. "Won Bok (Choi) is doing a good job caring for her and raising her up."

She nodded her head, grateful for this bit of information. How she longed to ask questions. How she longed to go help her daughter, but she remained quiet.

He continued, "Now I have some directions to give you. I must ask that, from this time, you stop thinking of her as your daughter. You raised her. You offered her to Heavenly Parent. Now she is not really your daughter any longer." He looked at her intently. "Can you accept that?"

It would be hard for any mother to accept such a direction, but Soon Ae loved him and always obeyed him. Her very name meant "Obedient Love." It had been given to her by a minister.

"Yes, True Father," she said softly, without looking up. "I can accept that."

"Good," he said. "Then Won Bok Choi will be her mother from this moment on. Do you understand?"

"Yes," she answered. In her heart, maybe she could not fully understand everything, but she sensed that what he was asking was very important. At that moment, even though she was his mother-in-law, she felt like his child and her heart beat with love for her father. She was about to stand up to leave, when he added another surprising direction.

"Furthermore, from now on, I want you to stay away as much as possible," he said. "If you come to Sunday Service or any other activity, you should use the back door and sit in the back. Don't ask to see her—or me. Just go about your work in the kitchen and serve everyone humbly." He paused a moment and then added rather sternly, "And furthermore, you must never, never tell your daughter that she is to be pitied or that you wish she didn't have this position. If you ever speak like that, it will be the greatest crime. You will hurt her terribly—and you will hurt all women."

As she went about her duties in the days following, Soon Ae felt as though she had no family or friends anymore. She couldn't visit her child. The people in the church seemed to be uncomfortable around her and wouldn't look at her and some of them appeared even to dislike her. Why? What had she done? She was so lonely. Because of these difficulties, she often became sick. The stress affected her stomach, and she was in a lot of pain. For months on end, she could only eat a small bit of rice each day. She grew worn and thin.

The other women soon noticed how difficult her life had become, and before long they took pity on her.

"Look how she's treated," they said. "She's an outcast, a nobody. She has to come and go by the back door. She has no friends. No family. I wouldn't want to be in her situation, poor woman." Some of the women thought back to their spiteful words and regretted them.

Through these difficult years, Soon Ae focused on her love for Heavenly Parent and for True Parents. She thought about how she had been led to join the Holy Lord Christain Order and then to the Ho Ho Bin Christian group and then to True Father himself. As far as she knew, she was the only person to have been in all three of these groups that were considered providentially significant, and she knew God had been guiding her to all of them. Therefore, she would be faithful always. She would never give up!

No one could know at that point that it was important for Soon Ae to suffer and be rejected yet never complain. No one could explain it to her and make it easier for her to bear. It was a test that most women might have failed. Soon Ae trudged onward, shielding her faith like a candle in a high wind.

Many years later, True Father praised and honored Soon Ae Hong for her steadfast faith. True Father even gently teased her about how strict he had had to be with her in those early days. He would eventually give her the heavenly title of "Great Mother." But there was no hint of what was to come during those early difficult days back at Chung Pa Dong church.

Hak Ja Han's life, too, had completely changed overnight. One day she was quietly studying in Choon Cheon city; a month later, she was married to True Father. Now, everyone watched her to see if she would be a good wife and mother. Deep in her heart, she knew God had prepared her for this mission. Heavenly Parent had already taught her to deal with loneliness, to work hard, to persevere, and to keep herself pure and centered on God. She had also learned to love God's wondrous creation.

On the other hand, nothing could have prepared her for this new life. She was on her own. Her mother was not allowed to visit her.

Her husband was always with the church members or on the mountain praying or in his little room praying. His closest disciples were always around. She lived in a separate building, and once in a while True Father would visit.

Although no one said anything to her personally, she could feel jealousy from some of the women. She could feel eyes watching her; ready to criticize her if she failed. Not only did she feel rejected by many members, she also felt rejected by True Father. He never discussed things with her or chatted or shared his feelings with her. He didn't ask her opinion on anything. He didn't ask her how she was. Sometimes he would be warm and kind; the next day, he would be cold and tyrannical. In fact, he treated her more like a servant than a wife. Whenever True Father gave a lecture, she was expected to be there, but she had to enter by the back door and sit in the rear of the room. She shed many tears.

By early summer, she learned that she was going to have a baby. As the scorching heat invaded all corners of Korea, she hid her feelings of nausea and stayed active.

The food at that time was better than in the earlier days, but they still ate barley instead of rice most of the time. Every Korean knows that only very poor people ate barley, yet rice was too expensive for the church members. True Father insisted that they both should eat barley just like everyone else.

Whenever True Father traveled around in the jeep to visit the church members in other towns and in the countryside, she went along. Korean summers are always very hot and bouncing around in a dusty jeep with the wind in her face made it unbearable. The wind tried to blow through the lace sleeves of her Korean dresses, but there was no relief from the humidity.

Oh, how she missed her mother! If only she could go to her and cry and rest. She was constantly tired. And always, she felt overwhelming loneliness. Even the flowers of Cheju Island would have made her feel less lonely at that point. At least on that island, where she had experienced loneliness so many years ago, there weren't hundreds of eyes watching her all the time.

By and by, after the cold winds of winter blew in from the North, the time came for the birth of their first child. That day, December 11,1960 (by the lunar calendar), the baby was born. It was a girl, a little princess! Her name was Ye Jin. But was Mother congratulated? Probably not much, for the church members were expecting a boy. Korean culture in general held boys up much higher then they did girls. This was something that had not changed in Korean society yet. They were shocked that a girl was born first.

"You see?" some said. "She can't even produce a boy. She's failed."

After the first year of marriage, almost all of True Mother's time was centered on having babies, nursing, and taking care of babies and little children. She still traveled with True Father as much as she could, but many times she had to stay home.

Two years after her first child was born, on December 3, 1962, a second baby was born and it was a boy. Their first son. Two and one-half years later, another daughter and just one year and three months later another son.

When the seven years of their marriage ended, True Mother had given birth to four children and was already pregnant with the fifth.

After the first three years of marriage, True Mother moved into True Father's room in the Chung Pa Dong church. Now she wouldn't have to be alone so much. However, she soon realized that she had only traded the old problems for a new set of problems. They had one small room of their own. All they had to do was close the sliding door to have peace and quiet. Right? Unfortunately, it was not that simple. For one thing, the walls were so thin, you could hear everything in the rooms even when the doors were closed. Secondly, there were always people in the room talking to True Father until midnight, one o'clock, two o'clock in the morning and even later. Night after night, True Mother's body would be crying out for rest, but she couldn't pull out her mat and lie down on the floor when people were still in the room. Only when everyone had gone for the night and True Father had finished his prayers could she finally sleep properly.

After only two or three hours of sleep, however, True Father would bolt awake and call for one of his disciples. He was already thinking of the problems of the world. Sleep was finished for that night! Within a few minutes, True Mother had to be up and presentable because that was about how long it took for Mr. Eu or another disciples to come when they were called.

Meanwhile, Soon Ae was having dreams. Night after night, it was the same dream. Her daughter would come running up to her. She was in her nightgown, and her hair was flowing free in the wind. Soon Ae could see that she was very, very tired, and her eyes were red from crying. She would just collapse in her mother's arms and cry, "Oh, I'm so tired and sleepy!" When Soon Ae awoke, however, she was not allowed to go to her daughter to comfort her. She could only relive her dream in silence and cry in silence.

There were days when True Mother thought she couldn't continue. "Everyone thinks I should be perfect," she said to herself. "But, of course, I'm not. The standard for being True Mother is too high! It's almost impossible to achieve!"

While she was going through their first seven years together, no one explained to True Mother why she was being treated in such a terrible way. No one told her, "You see, True Father is making you suffer on purpose. There's a reason." No one said, "It won't be like this forever. Just hold on for seven years, and then things will be better." No one explained, "You have to start out from the very bottom, as a servant, before you can go to the top as True Mother."

As these years went by, there were some good moments for True Mother, too. The most wonderful part was that Heavenly Parent never forgot her, and He often came close to her to encourage her. She learned that when one goes through hardships, Heavenly Parent comes closest. God can't resist. Heavenly Parent is very drawn to lonely and suffering hearts, because His own heart has been so lonely and suffering for so very long.

Also, despite the complaints of some church members, there were many other people who were very kind to her and really tried to help. In this way, she learned how to experience both hardships and joy, rejection and love.

On December 31, 1967, True Mother's first seven-years with True Father was complete. True Father had treated her like a servant. He had treated her like a child. He had treated her like a younger sister. Through all these trials, she had totally sacrificed herself. She had given her total obedience to God; she had given her total love to her husband. She didn't let herself get discouraged and give up. She was completely obedient. And above all, she had never complained! She had grown to the point where she could be True Mother.

One day, True Father prayed in front of everyone, "Dear Heavenly Parent, please look at your beautiful daughter. She has succeeded. She suffered for seven years, but she is victorious. Please bless her now." Tears streamed down his face as he prayed, for it had hurt him terribly to make her suffer for seven years in order to properly raise her up. He'd had to be like the strictest of teachers, the strictest of fathers in order to make sure that this very young and inexperienced woman grew properly in her training, step by step. No one had realized how much pain he had felt in his own heart during that time.

The very next day, January 1, 1968, True Father announced the first True Heavenly Parent's Day—or God's Day. Not many people had understood the importance of True Mother's role in the creation of God's Day. After that, many people repented for the way they had treated True Mother.

"We are sorry we complained about her," they cried. "We can see that she is, indeed, our True Mother. We can see that she is the only bride for True Father. And we can also see that Soon Ae Hong must be respected."

True Mother remained quiet, pondering these things in her heart, and bearing no ill will towards anyone.

Though they had married seven years earlier, and Hak Ja Han had become True Mother in title, she had, seven years later, proven to all the cosmos that she had taken responsibility for herself and chose to stand, for the sake of all women before and after her, steadfast as the daughter of God. Now, she could stand with Sun Myung Moon, the True Father, as True Mother in name, heart, spirit and soul, and together become the True Parents of all humankind. Together they would go out into the world to teach Divine Principle to everyone and bring God's children back to Heavenly Parent.

Soon Ae Hong offered her beautiful daughter to God and though it pained her greatly, later on, she was honored as the "Great Mother." When God asks for someone or asks us to give something away, it is to make us more pure so that Heavenly Parent can give it back to us a hundred times over. Deep in their hearts, both Great Mother Hong and True Mother understood this and they followed with steadfast faith through a deep, dark tunnel into the light of glory.

www.ingramcontent.com/pod-product-compliance
Lightning Source LLC
Chambersburg PA
CBHW050634300426
44112CB00012B/1798